We hold on so tight to our memories, our ideals, our beliefs, our possessions, our relationships...

We hold on so tight that we can't let go and no one would dare try to pull them out of our grip! We own them; they are who we are and we are never letting go! Yet, at the point of death it will all be ripped away. The old cliché goes "you can't take it with you", so, why spend your whole life clinging to it?

Our lives are programmed from the moment we are born. We are given a name and off we go. Everything in every moment makes an impression whether or not we know it and these impressions mold us. My parents fell in love, married and had kids. They raised us by their own conditioning and programming that was handed down from their parents. They did what they felt was in the best interest for us kids. They followed the rules to a "T" and never questioned any of it. I feel like I have always questioned it. I don't blame anyone for anything, including my parents. Maybe Dad didn't say "I love you", but I have always felt loved. Maybe I felt he expected too much from me and in my younger years pleasing him was important to me. My point is quite simple. I have lived the life I have lived because I did! I rebelled against doing what I have been told to do and being who everyone has expected me to be. I took my own road. I just knew that I wanted to live this life and not get caught up in a trap. A resentful marriage, having kids, kids and more kids to complete me. Buying a house with that white picket fence that I would rot in, having the same nine to five job day in and day out. Paying the bills and putting a few bucks aside to take the kids on vacation and fighting the entire time! I have never wanted that kind of life for myself. I have gotten a lot of shit for not "settling down" but I have to tell you, I have had and am still having an awesome life!

Writing my memoir was interesting. It changed nothing. I had many sleepless nights, many conversations but in truth, it's done! Trying to figure out why I behaved the way I did does nothing for me, I just know, I know longer behave that way, some get it, some don't. It's doesn't matter, seriously, this story could have ended differently, but it didn't. If I were to make a point it would be to stop living in fear. Live how you dream it, not someone else's dream but yours and yes the journey gets weird, so what! You alone judge it, no one else really gives a shit.

I love my parents, and I love my family. We don't live the same but who cares? I don't. I know love is not about your wealth, your religion or your ideals. I am here and I plan on having some fun.

IF THE SHOE FITS

By Schelli Rothi

ISBN – 978-0-578-02753-1

It is important to me to take a moment and thank the love of my life! Mike has been by my side through this entire adventure. I started by translating all my journals. At first I was going to do more of a journal type memoir and as things go, that changed. I still spent a good year translating the journals and questioning all the content. I have asked Mike to read and listen over and over again. It has been as interesting three years. Mike has been incredible as I have worked my way through all the memories. Once you read "If The Shoe Fits" you will understand. I have never met another human being that is unconditional in every sense of the word. He really does love me!

Thank you Mike for not judging me. Without your support there is a pretty good chance I would never have finished, or even started! I love you!

Table of Contents

Preface

Throughout my life I have been carrying along with me a box filled with photo albums. I've carried it from apartment to apartment, state-to-state. Tucked away in this box are all of the memories, photos of all of the big events in my life: photos of my childhood and the trips I have taken; photos of my theater days; photos of my parents and grandparents; photos of friends and boyfriends. The box wasn't that big at first, but as the years passed the box got bigger and heavier. I was getting so tired of carrying my past around with me. I finally took that box, which took two people to carry, and threw it out! Yes, I threw out 40 years of photo moments and I never looked back.

My past is just that, my past. I was tired of living in it and carrying it around with me. I want to look at life new in every moment. I don't want to base a relationship from my past relationships. I don't want to hold on to things that don't serve me presently. "I will not live in the past"… if I had only done this sooner. I didn't do it that way and it is what it is. I can't keep pulling myself into past sadness and past joys! These feelings don't exist anywhere except in my head and that is enough! It's done!

I have spent most of my life doing what I had to do to fit in. I had become this robot going through the motions. I was a parrot repeating everything I heard; I was a living zombie. On the outside I appeared fine but on the inside I was a mess! I had big dreams that someone always managed to smash, and piece-by-piece I became numb. I became numb to everything! It's true, you know, that when you hit rock bottom you have nowhere else to go but up. I rode that rollercoaster for a very long time but I eventually got off. I realized that I created everything. I was and am responsible for this life and when it really hit me, it hit me hard, and instead of talking the talk I walked the walk. Now I'm running!

I have let go of what others may think or feel about me. I don't want to be influenced by other people's thoughts and ideas on what is wrong and right. I feel that what is, is; there is nothing more to it!

I told my dad that I was writing this and he said, "Why would anyone want to read your book? You're not rich and famous, and you're not interesting." I guess we will just have to see about that.

If the Shoe Fits…

Chapter One

I was born in Oak Lawn, Illinois and soon after my birth we moved to Kalamazoo, Michigan. I don't have any memories of my birthplace. My parents had two boys before I came into the world and once they had their little girl they were done. I love my parents, but I am sure at times I didn't feel that way. They both worked full time; my mom worked her whole life at Upjohn's and took an early retirement. Mom was always supportive, she backed me on all the things that I wanted to do. I was a tap dancer for many years. I took voice lessons and loved to audition for musicals. Mom was always in my corner, yet she often reminded me that I couldn't get the lead in everything. When I came home crying because the boys at school were calling me "Schelli smelly" and throwing worms at me, Mom was always there to comfort me as best she could. She would say, "the next time they call you 'Schelli smelly' you just tell them, 'at least you smell good'." I used to laugh at this, thinking how it was not the comeback I wanted to use. Mom has a heart of gold. She is one of the most giving and unconditional people I know. My mother fully believes that once you get married you stayed married through thick and thin. That is exactly what she did. Mom is a Christian woman, she believes in the story completely.

11

Every Sunday without fail we were forced off to Church. It was Mom's doing, not Dad. I would guess he just went to keep her quiet, but he often didn't go because his church was on the golf course.

Mom is really quite simple yet, she stresses a lot and I mean a lot. My dad is a bit more complicated; Dad is the kind of guy that kept it all inside. The first time I saw my dad cry was when his dad died. That was the first time. I was, I think, around 19. We sat at my grandpa's bedside and watched him take his last breath. That was a moment in my life that I will never forget.

I really didn't get into much trouble when I was young, just the typical things. Mom was never the one to do the punishing, it was always "just wait till your dad gets home," and that of course scared the shit out of me. Dad would get the belt out. I remember one time my brother, Wilson, dipped his hands in the pudding Mom had made for dinner. When mom asked who did it of course Wilson would not confess, so when dad came home he put us back to back in chairs and we had to sit there until one of us confessed. Being the only girl and the youngest I was always bullied into a confession for something I didn't do. This ended with me saying I did it and Wilson going off to play while I got the punishment. Another time my oldest brother, Robert, had turned the heat way up in the house and my dad demanded to know who did it. All three of us were put in our rooms and both Wilson and Robert walked past my door saying that if I didn't say I did it they would kick my ass. Once again I owned up to something I didn't do, and this went on and on for years until I started to stand up for myself. I think that Dad knew all along who did it, yet that didn't seem to matter.

I remember falling out of a tree when I was about 5. I was playing with my friends; I couldn't talk them into climbing up the tree and they wanted to go home, so I climbed up there by myself. I was almost to the top when my foot got stuck between two branches. I yelled at Lynn, one of my friends, to go get someone to help me down. She ran off and never came back. I sat there forever until I managed to get my foot loose. I started to bring myself down and snapped a weak branch. I lost my balance and fell to the cement. I don't remember the fall but I do remember lying there afterwards. I couldn't move, my head was turned towards the road. My eyes had to have been open because I remember seeing my mom drive by in her yellow bug and all I could think about was getting into trouble for being barefoot. Next thing I remember is Mom screaming and Wilson running out. They dragged me into the car and took me to the hospital. The doctor said that I had a concussion and that we should be glad I wasn't dead since I cracked my head open. I liked being in the hospital because they brought me popsicles, yet every time I ate one it made me throw up. I didn't care. I just kept eating them. After I got out of the hospital, the doctor said that I had to be very careful to not fall on my head or it could kill me. From that accident on, my brothers had to leave me alone. If they even came close to popping me in the head they were in big trouble. I used this in my favor for many years until Robert said, "enough of this head injury crap, it's not going to work anymore." They were back to picking on me.

I vaguely remember one other accident, and maybe I only have the memory because I have been told the story so often: This happened when my brothers were in little league. I was out running around, having a grand old time, when I ran right into a guy who was doing batting practice. He swung that bat right into my face, knocking my teeth and I out! I guess that was pretty traumatic for the parents. I just remember being rushed to the hospital to get my popsicles. I lost my baby teeth, so the big ones grew right in, and there I was, a little girl with big buckteeth. I was teased quite a bit and I hated that. I never had kids of my own and I never really wanted to. I can only imagine what we as kids put our parents through; maybe that's one reason I never wanted kids. I honestly never thought too much about it, it just never appealed to me. What did appeal to me was being successful and making money; this, I'm sure came from Dad's influence.

My dad would get so disgusted with me. I wasn't the kind of girl that was quiet and polite, I was a bit loud and would speak out. I would burp and fart with no problem and he would always shake his head saying, "It's no wonder you don't have a boyfriend."

Maybe I was outspoken because I was always told to not talk back. I wasn't allowed to think for myself. My opinion did not matter. This never made much sense to me, why couldn't I have my own feelings about something? When I was little, I hated mushrooms because they were ugly but I was forced to eat them; I couldn't leave the table until I ate everything on my plate. I tried everything to get out of this but nothing ever worked. If I tried pushing the peas under my plate, eventually they were found and I was in trouble again. I recall sitting at the dinner table one night when we were living on Eagle Lake in Michigan. I must have been around 13 or 14. I can't remember what we were talking about but I remember my Dad saying not to talk back to him. I couldn't let it go. I challenged him and before I knew what was going on he was up and out of his chair with me up against the wall with his hand around my neck! Then he sent me off to my room, where I couldn't come out until I was ready to shut my trap!

I had the best bedroom in the house. It was downstairs, away from everyone else. I loved our house on the lake. It had 5 bedrooms and two kitchens. One kitchen was in the basement and I liked to fantasize that it was my own kitchen; that it was my own apartment, and it kind of was. I had my own bathroom, kitchen and bedroom. I had it going on at that age. I even had my own princess phone. Dad would play silly tricks on me all the time. If I went to use the bathroom and left the bedroom light on for just two minutes, he would take my light bulbs. If I left clothes on the floor, he would collect them and hide them; one time I found a whole handful of my clothes in the trunk of his car! One night I was just about to fall asleep when the door came bursting open and he ran through my room hitting the floor with a newspaper. I snapped upright and watched in wonder to what he was doing. He then stood up and said, "Oh well, can't find the mouse," walked out and shut the door behind him. I was up all night thinking about that damn mouse and it crawling all over me in the middle of the night. Dad had a great sense of humor and we were teasing each other all of the time; we still do today. I say the mouse never existed, and when I ask him about it today, he doesn't even remember! I sure do!

Money and prestige were pretty important to my dad. He was pretty high up in the banking world. He did all of the financial stuff and he did it really well. I always looked up to my dad. I even tried to follow in his footsteps, but that just wasn't my thing; I was more creative and the money world just didn't work for me. I often felt my dad was disappointed in me. I couldn't seem to do anything right in his eyes. Dad never said, "I love you" or showed much affection yet I loved him no matter. He really was a great dad and always looked out for my best interest. Dad was a corporate man; he despised gossip, he wasn't really religious. He followed the rules. He was not one to travel. It was just work, work and more work. He has bailed me out more times than I can count, and he took notes. The money he gave me was always to be paid back and it was.

17

My brothers and I are all so different. The first-born is Robert; he was very protective of me when I was little yet as time passed and he got older, he also got meaner. I can remember so many occasions where he would lock up the house and not even let me in after school. My friends and I were terrified of him. Robert was a wild one. He got into drugs quite young and got into a lot of trouble. He was always in fights, either at school or at home with Wilson and I. He was totally rebellious and split the school scene at a young age, running off to Florida. One time after school I came home and found Robert bent over the kitchen sink with a knife carving into his wrist. He was crying and saying he was not going to go to jail, that he would kill himself first. I was trying to get him to stop. There was blood everywhere and he kept slicing away into his wrist. Finally, Mom came home; he put the knife down and walked away. Trying to take his life became a pastime for Robert. I can't tell you how many nights he would call me saying he was going to do it, kill himself, and I would spend forever trying to talk him out of it. His favorite attempt method was the wrist; I believe the marks are still there today. Robert was a violent guy. He drank way too much and spoke his mind at all of the wrong times. I remember one story where he was at a party: he made a sexual comment to this guy's girlfriend and went and sat back down.

18

Before he knew it, the guy whose girlfriend it was kicked him right in the face. The kick shattered all of the bones in his face and he ended up in the hospital. Robert has told me many stories. I don't really know how many of them are true, yet the shattered face was evidence.

Robert has never been married, and can't seem to keep a girl for very long. He looks at a woman as a piece of ass, and that's it. Once in the middle of the night I remember he had a friend over. I remember seeing this guy enter my bedroom, light a match and then come towards me, I grumbled and rolled away and he left. That really freaked me out. Robert wasn't around much and my parents ended up kicking him out of the house. I don't talk to Robert that much as of the present. He has lived in Florida forever. It's the same story; he's in and out of places, sleeping on the beach with no money, no nothing. He appears quite happy about all of it. Robert is not religious at all and he is not atheist either. I really think he is more into "energy" and "alien" stuff, it just depends on if he's drinking or not. I love my brother; he lives as he chooses.

Wilson and Robert don't get along at all, and that could have something to do with the God thing. They did get along when they were younger but we all went our own way. Wilson is really creepy with his God perception and Robert will have nothing to do with it. Wilson and I did more things together as kids. We did the camping trips with Grandma and Grandpa. Wilson and I hung out more; Robert wasn't around that much. I used to feel sorry for Wilson. He was such a nerd in school. He just didn't fit in and was teased a lot. He was teased about being gay, always getting picked on. To this day he believes that being gay is a sin and that homosexuals will burn in hell. He has a major issue with gays. I recall one day after school: this guy kept threatening that he was going to kick Wilson's ass once we got off the bus. Sure enough, we got off the bus and this guy starts wailing on Wilson. I couldn't stand it so I grabbed my crutches and beat this guy on the back until he let Wilson go. If Robert had still been around you can bet this never would have happened. Poor Wilson, he was really a good guy. He was really into helping people; he volunteered for the fire department. One morning when the fog was really bad, a girl from school was hit by the school bus. Wilson was first on the scene. The girl was torn apart but still alive. He talked about this later on, how he had to pick up her body parts. She died later that day in the hospital.

Another time at our house on Eagle Lake, a big boat ran right over the top of a small fishing boat and cut this guy's neck so deep his head could have come off. Wilson was, again, first on the scene. Wilson gave the guy mouth to mouth, but he also died. Wilson was truly a caretaker and he followed that to a career. Today Wilson is a nurse; he's a bit anal but that's his thing.

Wilson never borrowed a penny from my parents. He always made his own way. He met a girl from the paper dating service and soon after they were married. I would guess that my parents have put more money out for Robert than for Wilson or myself. My dad really tried everything to get Robert on track. He would pay to bring Robert home though soon he was off again, after he trashed the place my dad paid for. He did this over and over again until my dad finally said "no more!"

Chapter Two

My parents moved the family out to Mattawan when I was in fourth grade. Leaving my best friend Lynn was hard for me, though I soon made other friends; but Lynn and I always kept close. My mom and Lynn's mom were great friends, so Lynn came out to the lake often. I didn't stay at her house that much. Lynn had an interesting house life. Her home was a nightmare. There was shit piled everywhere, up to the ceiling; I guess you could say that they liked to keep everything. I remember at one time they had around fourteen dogs and their entire basement was nothing but shit and pee piles. I never felt comfortable in their house. They even put their gum on the dresser. Oh, did I hate that. I don't chew gum and I never have. My mom says that when I was really little, before I could talk, my brothers would put their gum on the table at dinner and I would point at it and scream. My mom had to cover the gum with a napkin and I would stop screaming.

I really loved growing up on the lake, it was so much fun. We had boat parties. It was just a good experience. I lived on this so-called island, there was one small road that took you all the way to the end where I lived and the road was surrounded by water. All of the kids on Treasure Island (that was the name of our road) would have their mischief. I may have been one of the biggest rebels. A neighbor boy that was in my grade had one of the hottest looking Dads! I had such a crush on this guy that I would sneak over to their house and peek in the windows at him. Sometimes I would catch him on the sofa with just his underwear on. When my friends came over to stay the night we would sneak out and break into his home and steal wine. He used to have cases and cases of cheap wine and I figured he wouldn't miss a bottle or two. The house next to ours was more of a summer home and they had this boathouse. We would break into that boathouse to drink and smoke. I also remember always finding ways to make money and I would always talk a friend into going into the scam with me. I loved eating Jello raw from the box and when Mom didn't have any in the cupboard I would go to the neighbors and borrow a box saying it was for mom. I would eat the whole box, then fill the box with sand and return it. I used to knock on doors and say I was collecting money for the church and then pocket all the cash. I was always coming up with something, being the entrepreneur that I am today. I hated school. My first day at school I got in a fight with this girl and from then on I always struggled with fitting in. I didn't have many friends; the ones I did have were, of course, superficial. I don't think anyone knows how to be a friend at that age. I was in and out of fights a lot with these girls for some stupid "he said, she said" shit. I honestly don't have much to say about my school days. I found every reason possible to not have to go though I was still forced to; forced to learn things I knew I would never use in the real world. I tried out for cheerleading a couple times and finally got accepted in ninth grade. For once I actually felt popular, but I hated the whole cheerleading persona and never tried out again after that football season. I never had a boyfriend in school; most of the guys I hooked up with were not in my school, usually older boys from other schools or out of school. The guys in my school just didn't care much for me, I feel more that it was an intimidation thing. Even then I was a pretty vocal girl. I wasn't one to sit back and do what I was told.

My school friends consisted of Linda, Mandy, Mary and a few others that didn't stay close friends. Those three are the ones that have played a bigger role in my life.

I was a risk taker. I loved to make crank calls and I got plenty of them myself. Once, this guy called me. He sounded nice and he was telling me about this study they were doing at a college. He asked if I would like to participate. The study had something to do with spankings and I knew it was a joke but I wanted to go. I wanted to see what would happen. I was driving at this point and still in school. I remember it being cold and snowing like crazy the night I decided to check out this guy's story. I told a friend what I was doing just in case something happened to me. I drove about thirty minutes out into the woods somewhere and found the guys house. I went in and he offered me some wine. He was an older guy. I recall walking into the living room and taking a peek into his bedroom. I saw handcuffs and rope on the bed. I was a bit nervous but played the part. All he wanted was for me to spank him. I brought along some ping-pong paddles because the "study" was on spanking. He didn't want to spank me, that, I am glad for. He just wanted me to spank his naked ass, so I did. I wailed on him and he loved it! This was new to me and I knew I had to make a break for it. I did get out of there. I can't remember how, but I did and that's all that mattered.

I can't remember when I started to get into boys; it must have been when Linda and I became friends. Linda was the kind of girl that I wanted to be. She was trashy, yet popular. She lost her virginity pretty young and she seemed to be experienced. She and I were tight for a long time. We were

25

at each other's houses all of the time. We did discos and the roller rink.

That was our fun; boys were always involved. The boys always liked her

better than me. Being with her was good enough for me. We had more

freedom at her house. She manipulated her parents into doing whatever

she wanted and if they said no, we would just sneak out. We use to climb

out of her bedroom window, steal the car and go have some fun. We also

use to sneak the boys into her room and we would lie on the same bed and

make out together. That came to an end when we got busted at her house.

The boys were climbing out of the window when Linda's sister saw them

and told her parents. The boys were caught. We acted totally stupid about

it. Linda's parents didn't buy it, though, and I was sent home. I snuck out

of my house all of the time, either with Linda, with someone else or alone.

I was in it for the thrill; and it was thrilling! Since I had the bedroom in the

basement, I would wait for my parents to go to bed and I would sneak out

the door. They never knew this for a long time. I would have boys that

could drive wait for me at the bottom of the hill, and once all was clear I

was outta there until dawn. I was out smoking pot, hash, drinking it up;

but not giving it up, not yet. One time I remember sneaking into Wilson's

room and stealing his car keys. Linda and I had it all planned: we snuck

out and stole his car for the night only to meet up with this guy so Linda and him could get it on. I really liked this guy, but he was all about Linda; not me, never me. The next morning on the way to church, (yes, I was still being forced to go to church) the neighbor was out investigating the railroad ties that we pulled up to get the car out. We didn't know how to put the car in reverse, so whatever we did we had to be sure that we didn't have to back up. She and I laughed forever about that. We never got caught, so we kept on doing it. We would steal gas from the neighbors; whatever we could to sneak out and it all was so perfect until…

Writing notes back and forth in school was the greatest. A friend and I were planning our big sneak out; it was no big deal, no boys, just us sneaking out and roaming the neighborhood. Well, when she got home, she left our notes on her bed and her mom found them. That night it was all set for us to sneak out. I stuffed the bed, kept the radio on low and ventured out. She and I met up and were just walking when I saw car headlights, so we ditched behind a tree. The car came around the corner and slowed down until it stopped. Next, I hear "Schelli, come out." Holy shit it was my dad again, "Schelli, come out." I told Chris to step out so he wouldn't think it was me. She steps out and my dad says, "Oh, sorry, I thought you were Schelli." He was just about to leave when he turned and said, "Who is behind the tree with you?" Busted! I got my ass whipped that night. I found out later how it unraveled. Chris' mom called my dad and told him about the notes. He didn't believe that I would do such a thing, but after much pushing he finally pulled back the sheets to discover I was gone. You know the rest of the story. The best part of this story was my Dad insisted on taking Chris home and made her get in the car. She told him where she lived and we pulled up in the driveway. The thing was, it wasn't her home! He said he was going to wait until she was in the house. I was freaking out! She walked right up to the door and right into this house! Later I found out that she stepped into the stranger's house and squatted down by the door until we left. She said people were awake downstairs and she was scared to death! She got out of that thinking that her parents knew nothing. Not the case.

I believe that was the end of my sneaking out days. By then I was getting older and was doing what I wanted anyway. Life went on that way, getting in and out of trouble. Boys, boys, boys; they became my fascination.

What was wrong with me? I couldn't seem to get a guy that would stick around. Mandy and I were good friends for most of our school days until I met this guy and introduced them. One day I called Mandy and he answered the phone, so that's how I found out that they were together. I was so hurt and couldn't forgive her for going behind my back. That ended our friendship for a few years. Mandy grew up in a trailer park. Her parents were divorced. I guess you could say she was "poor" compared to my family, yet I never looked at it that way. I don't think my Dad cared much for Mandy then; after all she didn't come from money, just a mom that bitched about everything. Mandy would stay at my house more than I at hers, but it was fine when I stayed with her. I guess it was that her mom could give a shit what we did, so I felt free. We could stay up all night and eat what ever we could find, that was usually potted meat.

Mandy and I had many great times out doing our thing. She puked in my first car, a Ford EXP. We had many photo sessions, thinking we could be models. I loved Mandy, and again we were young and would learn much on our journey. We didn't regain our friendship until after we graduated. I was a counselor at a camp and knew she would be a good counselor as well, so I called and got her the job. Soon we came to an understanding and became friends again.

I should mention Mary for a moment. Although Mary and I were friends in school, we became better friends afterwards. Mary was a year younger than me, yet we clicked somehow. She and I did some stupid shit together. I think I influenced her more. Her parents didn't care too much for me. I would do anything to keep her out longer with me: like running the gas tank dry, which was a good excuse for being late. I remember this school project in Select Choir where I had to sell this stupid shit and get points to win this even more stupid stuffed animal. I talked her into going door to door with me. We would present this big box of stupid shit and sell it. The person would fill out a form and give us money, all good right? Except I never delivered the goods. I took the cash, cashed it and never went back. She and I would go buy a burger at Burger King. I actually won that contest and the big over stuffed puffball animal.

I was a great liar and a great manipulator. I could make up any story and people would believe me. My parents were clueless to my behavior. They trusted me even when I got busted for things. I took a trip with a friend to North Carolina and met this boy there. He was older, and a total rebel, but I had a crush and wanted him to come back to Michigan. I'm not sure how I got away with this one but my parents agreed to let him live with us. My dad got him a job and took him to work. I was still in school and was starting to feel weird about him living in our house. I would wake up sometimes and he would be sitting by my bed staring at me. It was creepy and eventually I got him kicked out of the house. I liked him one day and didn't the next; he grew tired of my childish behavior and got himself a girlfriend. I wanted him, but I didn't. I surely didn't want him to have a girlfriend, though. My feelings were all messed up. It finally exploded and my parents asked him to leave. I was a mental mess when it came to boys, friendships, all of it! All of the drama that I thought would never end!

Chapter Three

I lost my virginity in ninth grade! My parents never knew and afterwards I just carried on looking for love. I was always looking for love and never finding it. Just one night stands and drunk, fucked up nights that I would cry over time and again.

It was during the day. I took the paddleboat across the lake. Linda and a few friends were house sitting. My memory is dim. I remember going out for beer with this guy that they invited over, he was old enough to buy. I got in the backseat with him and Linda drove. I wish I could remember more. What I do remember is him taking an interest in me, and us kissing and fondling until my pants were down. Before I knew what was happening he was slamming his dick inside of me. I remember him asking if I had protection and at that time I didn't even know what protection was. I just said yes and in he went, full force. It did hurt and I just laid there, not sure what to do or how to feel. All of this happened as Linda drove through the parking lot of the skating rink. Here I was, getting laid for the first time and this is what I would remember. It was all set up. See, my friends thought it was time for me to lose my virginity and I was so confused I didn't know what to do; so it happened, my big sexual experience where I felt nothing. I cried for days. I paddled home and that night I was in so much pain. I crawled in bed with Dad. Mom was in the hospital having a hysterectomy. I woke up the next morning with blood all over the bed. My parents only thought I started my period. I knew the truth and from that day on I had to find a way to understand it.

My dog Smokey I had since birth died. This was pretty traumatic for me. I remember hearing from my room my dad saying, "He is dead; there is nothing we can do." I walked out into the living room and there he was, dead! I didn't understand. I loved that dog! I still don't understand, what is death? What is this death of virginity? That also traumatized me. I am no longer a virgin. Now what? It wasn't good, should it have been? What now? So many weird sexual things as a kid; I was so young. I didn't understand any of it. The kids in the neighborhood always teased me. We would go swimming and my neighbor would pull off my top. I liked it, I did; I liked the attention. The girls hated me and would talk so meanly about me. I really just wanted the boys to like me, but they never did, not really. They would just fuck with me and make me look like a fool, and a fool I was to ever allow that shit.

My parents never talked to me about boys. They never talked to me about love or about sex. I'm not sure why, it just didn't happen. Boys were pretty much the big topic for me at this point. I filtered through many boys, and I mean many, to find just one that would really care about me. They always say you remember your first kiss, your first love! I can't remember my first kiss but I will never forget my first love. Talk about being obsessed! Day and night I spent thinking about this guy. I ate, drank and slept thinking about him. I met Steve at a party when I was still in school. I use to go to his apartment all of the time at first. He was a bit older than me and I was totally head over heels for this guy. I was really just a piece of ass for him and he made a lot of promises that he never kept. He did manage to keep me sitting by the phone, endlessly waiting for him to call. I cried many nights over this guy and sometimes thought suicide was the only answer. Of course, a new guy would enter my life and I would be distracted for a while until that fell apart. Then I was back on Steve again. Not sure at what point I finally did get over him, but I know at that time it felt like forever. Here is a small example from my diary to give you a feel for what was going on with me then:

It has been four days since I have been with Steve. I wish he'd call! How long do I have to keep trying? I went to see two movies tonight with Mandy. God I'm lonely, I need to be loved. I need to love someone! I have to be positive that some day I will get love in return. I am tired, tired of loving Steve so much and getting no love from him. I need him---how long will the hurt last this time? Will I wake up tomorrow, happy? Maybe I won't wake up at all, maybe I'll just sleep my life away. How can I even face tomorrow when I feel like such a loser? There has to be some hope out there for me...somewhere. One week today and still no call! Damn you to hell for doing this to me. Doesn't he realize? Does he even care? I remember it all like it was two hours ago. I have to have him and if I can't then I'll lie down and die. How can some one have so much yet have nothing? Call damn you! Make me smile and laugh, I love you more than anyone. All the times we've been together I've put up my pride to be with him time and again. I keep running for him and not even realizing that he's using my love for his loneliness. My job isn't appealing anymore, nothing is. Steve, you were put in my life for a reason, for me to be hurt and for you to be satisfied? For me to realize how much of a fool I really am? Or for you to fall in love with me and I be with you and happily ever after? What reason could it be? We have made memories, but not long lasting ones. Only nightly ones that end when you close the door and I *drive home. Then I wait a few months...etc...We used to be together a lot, until well, he wanted a rest. After that, it's only when I call! He used to call me four times a week and I'd be on cloud nine. Now I'm in reality alone, and deeply in love! With him not even caring. Lines, hell, he's good at making you believe. Hell, he's an actor. Saying he wants a relationship was only a line, he don't give a shit and yah know, neither should I. I LOVE HIM! But should I fight for him forever? I've already lost my pride, what else can I lose? Steve---DAMN YOU TO HELL!!!*

I'm really fucked up. All I can think of is Steve--why hasn't he called? Here I am making spaghetti and damn I'm fucked up. I've been with Tracy all night kissing him. I can barely remember. I want Steve! Mother fucker call me now! I'm fucked! Forgive me- Steve- I love you! I called- hello, hello - click- call me- I can't get over you! God if I can't have you, give me death. I love you Steve I NEED YOU! YOU CALL

I got caught up in taking speed in high school; I bought in by the thousands just to get through another day. "Tombstones" was their name. I was taking these like candy. One night, staying at a friend's, I was feeling really awful. I can't even explain the pain today. Finally Annette's mom called my dad in the middle of a snowstorm and said it was pretty bad and he had to come and get me. Annette and I called the neighbor first, looking for something to make me throw up. Funny but he had something and when we went to get it, he couldn't find it. It turns out that if I had taken it, my stomach would have exploded. I had Appendicitis! The entire drive to the hospital my dad kept telling me I was being dramatic. Well he was surprised when they rushed me into the emergency! The doctor talked to me about the speed and I found out that speed does not digest. Oh, so that's the problem!

Lynn ended up getting married soon after I graduated. She was only eighteen and she already had one kid from another guy that split on her. Now, she finally found someone that would take care of her.

I knew it was time to move out on my own. Mandy and I were friends again and we decided to rent an apartment together. The first one we found ended up being condemned after we were partially moved in, so we waited it out and finally found a place in downtown Kalamazoo.

Having my own apartment was so much fun. It was not so much fun with

Mandy though. I was much more of a social bug than her. She had the domestic thing down pretty good and that just wasn't my thing. I would rather go out all night to the bars and bring home strangers. I wanted to drink until I couldn't see straight and, of course, have my pity parties. When we moved in, we didn't have much for furniture so my dad decided to buy this old crap he found at a garage sale. The chairs were all stained up and it was just ugly stuff. I didn't want to hurt Dad's feelings, so I acted excited and accepted the furniture. Mandy was livid, she even cried about this shit furniture. She insisted it go in the closet and we were to only pull it out if my parents came over to visit. She was so neurotic to me at that time, constantly following me around and cleaning up after me. This drove me nuts. She was obsessed with being married with children, cleaning and cooking. I just wanted to have fun and some furniture to sit on while I was doing it! I won't mention all of the guys that would be silly and a bit confusing. They came and went pretty fast in my world. I never knew how to be or who to be. My first experience with a black man had me fucked up for a while. This guy was really nice yet I couldn't get it out of my head that black and white don't mix, at least not as boyfriend and girlfriend. I never felt comfortable with it. All this fucked up programming from my younger years of being told who to date and who to be seen with. I even dated an Iranian and that was a nightmare. My dad wasn't too hip on the idea, but Mom never seemed to judge. The Iranian was really pushy with the sex and eventually I drove him away! Before, I did though he was kind enough to leave with me a nice reminder of him. Herpes!

One morning after staying the night, Mandy was driving her boyfriend home and was in a car accident that totaled her car. At the same time, I was being fired from my job. We decided it was time to throw in the towel and move back to my folks. She and I already had a hard time making ends meet and now it was just going to get worse. I always had my parents to fall back on, but her parents were pretty much non-supportive and non-existent. So we talked about it, packed up our trash and moved back home.

Chapter Four

I started a new job in a factory. I knew that I didn't want to rot in a factory so I told myself when taking the job that I would be out in one year. I would save enough money so I could start pursuing my dream. I actually did it too, but I still had to endure one year of hell working with blue-collar people that had no dreams and no imaginations. The people I never wanted to be like or be around. I took a deep breath and went for the ride; the ride that got me into crystal meth, married men, female jealousy and even more drama.

Working third shift was a killer so I was introduced to coke and crystal meth. I am a pretty upbeat personality so these drugs were a big hit with me, and an expensive one. I ended up introducing Mandy to Brian who worked at the factory and they eventually were married; she was only 19. I was really pissed at her for selling herself short. Once she was married and moved out I went about my own business with Mandy out of the picture. My parents would pay for most of the wedding, not to mention putting money down on Mandy and Brian's new house. I wasn't too happy about all of that, but I had other things going on in my life. Soon Mandy would be married; I just didn't have any interest in that settled down state of mind.

When I saw Darin for the first time I felt my heart race. He had the most stunning blue eyes I had ever seen. We played the flirting game for a while and he then finally asked me out. Darin wasn't interested in a relationship; he already had one, and a little girl to go along with it. I was still drawn to winning him over and tried endlessly to get him to fall for me. We did a lot of partying together, and had a lot of sex as well. Felica and I started hanging out together. She and I did a lot of drugs together and when we were really desperate for some meth and couldn't get our hands on any we would smash up speed and snort that. One night we were out at the bar all night and went back to Darin's. He and I got into an argument and he told Felica and me to leave. We were pretty messed up and he didn't seem to care. I actually turned around and begged him to let me stay since I was so drunk. He refused and sent us out into the night driving drunk. I was on the highway and so out of my head I couldn't keep the car on the road. I decided to pull over in the middle medium and have Felica drive. I had no sooner than pulled over when a cop was up on me! I went through the motions of repeating the alphabet and I decided to give it to him in song. It was at the Q that I lost it…Q L R O S…"Oh, let me do it again, I forgot the song!" Then he made me walk the crooked line. I tried flirting but that wasn't working. It was good cop, bad cop. One cop said they should just take us home and the other one said no way, we needed to learn a lesson. They handcuffed me and put me in the back of the cruiser. Instantly, the door was jerked open and Felica was yelling, "Run, Schelli, run!" I didn't run and I didn't learn my lesson, it took many years before I figured that out. So, I spent the night in jail. I made my one phone call to my dad. He told me to rot and hung up on me. It turned out that Brian and Mandy came to get me the next day. The outcome: I lost my license for 6 months, did one day of community service (because they liked me) and put out the almighty dollar! It always ends up being about money. The truth is that they could give a shit about me.

After that adventure I decided I needed to stay clear of Darin for a while. We hooked up on and off for the sex, but that was about it. When I worked at the factory, I lost a lot of weight and I was looking pretty good. I didn't have any problem hooking up with really great looking guys. The other "first time thing" I remember is my first threesome.

I met this guy from high school that was a few years older than me. We would get together often, but it was only for sex. One night we hooked up at this party (whenever I ran into him at a party, I was sure to get laid). He took me over to *Duck's Landing* (this use to be a hot tub place). His friend owned it, so we got in and had the whole place to ourselves. I remember being in the tub with him and we were kissing and caressing when I felt another hand on me. One thing worked into another and I decided to just go with the flow. It was an experience. One other time Felica wanted to give her husband the gift of a threesome and I agreed. This time it didn't go as well. Felica ended up leaving the room because her husband was more into me than her. I kept telling her to think about this before we went through with it. This little escapade ended our friendship; she just couldn't get over it. They ended up having a kid at some point and I'm pretty sure they ended up in divorce. Threesomes worked pretty good when it was two guys and myself, but the minute another woman was involved there was jealousy.

My days in the "factory" were long and tiring. All I did was party! Ken and I started seeing each other when he was married. He had two young boys and lived in a dumpy trailer. I was still at home but he and I would sneak around to see each other. I was seeing other guys as well, but none that I really cared about like Ken. I'm not sure why I fell so hard for Ken. He was a controlling, mean guy. Maybe that is why. I was always drawn to guys that treated me like shit. I just didn't get it. Ken eventually got divorced and I started shacking up with him. I hadn't moved in with him yet, because I had made plans to move to Detroit and go to broadcasting college. June 16th I turned 20 and I was really feeling like it was time to get moving with my life. Jeff, an old boyfriend, took me out for my birthday. He took me to this dive motel for sex. I was fine with that, Jeff and I always had a good time together and it was really all about the sex. What sucked was he snuck out when he thought I was sleeping and left me there. That, like so many nights, really hurt. I was tired of being hurt yet I kept putting myself in these positions. At this time, taking responsibility for my actions was something I couldn't or didn't do; it was always someone else's fault.

I finally did the research and enrolled in a broadcasting college in Detroit. I was so excited to go, yet worried I would lose Ken. My career was important but not as important as the boys. I had a few months before I finished out at the factory, which was good; the rumors and the gossip are unbearable at a factory. Mandy was getting married soon and I wanted to throw her a party. Mom and Dad went and got a hotel so we could have the party at the house. I hired a male dancer and boy did that get out of hand. He was a fine looking man and when he got there the bodyguard asked me to come into the bathroom to settle up. I didn't know he was going to ask me for a blowjob. I didn't do it. He ended up taking all of his clothes off and putting a towel around his waist, going from girl to girl as he slid the towel around her head so they could suck him off in private. I thought this was disgusting, I never touched his dick but half the women there did. I ended up fucking the bodyguard in the bathroom after the party. We all got pretty fucked up that night. Mandy of course was a good girl. It was years later when I heard that the dancer had gotten aids. Never heard if he died from it or not.

I finally moved to Detroit to begin my career in broadcasting. I found this apartment in Ferndale. The landlord was chief of police and when I was up looking for an apartment, I wandered into the police station asking for directions. I told them I was looking for an apartment and it turned out that the chief had one for rent. I lucked out, considering Ken and I had been looking for a place forever and we were running out of time before school started. This was a cute apartment and close to my school. The first week in Detroit, my mom came and stayed with me to keep me company and to help me get things in order. When she left, I was so depressed. I hadn't found a job yet and school was all I had going on. I was so bored and Ken of course had to check up on me constantly. He came up every single weekend and all that I remember is that we fought all the time.

The course was eight months long and I knew I didn't have enough money saved. I would have to find a job. I really loved broadcasting school; I was finally doing what I loved to do. It came really easy for me. It was for both Radio and TV, but I loved the TV part the most. I loved writing and producing mock commercials and learning to edit. The other kids in my class were great. I made many friends. Ken was always around, and I felt so obligated to him that I never ventured towards other guys. I had many chances and one night I came pretty close, but I just couldn't do it without the guilt. I befriended two guys at School; we hung out all the time. I had a huge crush on the one guy and fooled around with him a bit, but I never went to bed with him. I wanted to, but I couldn't forgive myself if I betrayed Ken.

School was great but I needed to bring in some cash, so I started to look for a job. I searched the papers for whatever I could find. One ad said "fitness training counter clerk." I thought this would be easy. I called the number and set up an interview. When I showed up to the address it had a really creepy feeling to it, but I went in anyway. I remember sitting there all suited up with these young girls walking around with hardly any clothes on. Their faces were all made up and I felt really stupid sitting there. This guy walks in and talks to the counter girl, "placing his order" so to say. One girl walks by and bends over; she has this tiny skirt on with no underwear! I thought at that moment I should run; but I couldn't, I was curious. So I was called to the back room. I walk down this long hall and enter this room. There is a big fat ass of a man sitting there, just eye balling me. I walk in and sit down. He takes one look at me and says, "do you know what you are applying for"? I say, "Yes." He says, "I don't think this is for you," so I say, "You're right." He was kind enough to let me go. I was so bummed! The paper ad was misleading. Here I was dying to get a job; any job, but not that kind of a job.

Eventually I did find a job at a phone company selling long distance service. I went through sales training, which I despised! How hard is it to sell long distance? Do I really need to sit through two weeks of someone telling me how to close a deal? I sell the way I sell, no one can tell me how to do it! I have always hated training. I hate meetings and anything that, to me, is just a waste of time. Throw me in and let me learn as we go! Anyway, I got through the training and actually did pretty well with selling, yet I hated sitting at a desk all day talking on the phone. Yawn.

My life consisted of work, school and Ken. I was getting really tired of it. When Lynn and Tom asked if they could come up and throw a party for this new thing they were involved in, I was more than happy to help. It was an art show and party combined. I typed up invitations and gave them out to everyone I wanted to come which was pretty much my entire class and a few select people that I worked with. There was one guy at work that kept harassing me, so I kept avoiding him but somehow the invite and directions to my apartment got into his hands. He never showed up on party night. The party was wild. We were all drinking and smoking. I remember going into the bathroom where Ken had some pot, he was a big pot smoker. He was rolling up a joint and this guy wanted to sprinkle some white stuff on it. I didn't have any interest so I passed but Ken wanted to try it. To this day I don't know what it was, but it made Ken extremely sick. He was throwing up green stuff. Everyone was just hanging, dancing and having a good time when this guy across the room screamed out, "I wanna get fucked!" and threw a beer bottle across the room. I was standing in the kitchen and the bottle came inches from my face. He got up and charged me. It took almost everyone in that room to bring him down. He was a guy in our class and the smoke must have gotten to him. We ended up putting him outside and told him to leave. He wouldn't leave; he just sat in his car and watched us. Eventually, he said, "Just kiss me and I will leave." He didn't say this to me; he said it to another guy. This other guy finally kissed him so he would leave. I don't think any of the class ever talked about it, whether he was actually gay or just fucked up. I know we all thought about it.

Weeks later, I was hanging alone at the apartment when a car pulled up. There was a knock at the door and it turned out to be this guy from work. He wanted to get me alone. I didn't think he presented any danger that I couldn't handle myself. He came in and started talking a lot of shit. He dumped a bunch of coke on my table and wanted me to party with him. I was freaking out since my landlord was a cop. I told him he should go, but he wouldn't. He started to grab me and force me to kiss him. I was fighting him off when my landlord pulled up! The guy got really paranoid, swept up his coke and headed for the door. The landlord never knew how he was actually my hero that day.

One of my teachers at school, the teacher that taught the video end of things, was telling me how he was a photographer and he would like to take shots for my portfolio. I fell for this right away. I knew I needed to get some head shots if I wanted to pursue acting. I decided I would go over to his house for the shoot. I have to be honest here that my memory on this night fails me. I really can't remember, or I have pushed it so far out of my mind that I choose not to remember. Maybe I do remember and I just can't come to admitting it. I want to say it happened like this: I got to his house, he offered me a drink, I accepted, and he drugged me without my knowledge. I have this weird feeling in my gut that I accepted the drug as well, that I knew deep down inside what was going to happen. The latter is hard to admit. I was drugged and that's for sure. He had the big screen set up and he had this porno type movie playing. I recall sitting on the couch and somehow he managed to get me into this chair where he tied me up. He stripped me naked and tied rope all around my body. I remember my tits being tied so tight and bulging. I sat there and watched this movie and he just talked and talked. He dropped his pants and wanted me to just watch him as he masturbated. That's all I can remember. I felt horrible, frozen; I could barely move I was so numb. He never raped me. He untied me and let me leave. I did all of this keeping my composure. On the inside I was a fucking mess. I missed days of work and eventually they fired me. I never did tell Ken, he would have killed him. I did mention it to some friends at school and I guess from what I heard he has done this to other students. He ended up getting fired, I just can't remember why.

I got another job as a cashier at a small store until school ended. When it did, I packed my shit and headed back to Ken to live with him in his small oven of a trailer. I did great in school. I graduated with a 4.0 GPA, which beats the 1.7 I got in high school. I knew if I wanted to work in the field of radio and television I had to move back to a market that I could begin in. Detroit was too big and honestly, I hated Detroit. There was so much crime; I never felt safe. I was in such a hurry to get back that I split on my lease early. I did all the right things, I wrote the letter and talked to the landlord directly and he said it was all good; all good until I received a letter from him saying he was keeping my deposit. I was really hurting for money and needed my deposit back. I went around and around with him on this. He even wanted the rent for the months I left on the lease. Bastard! What I found out at this point in my life is that you can't win when you are up against the law. You will always lose, and I did. He threatened to put me in jail! I remember sitting on the toilet in Ken's trailer reading the letter from him about going to jail if I failed to pay him. I was crying and crying. Ken came in and asked what all the crying was about? As I started to tell him, he said, "You will cry over a letter and over money but you never cry over the thought of losing me." I then cried some more! Selfish prick anyway.

I'm not sure why I felt so dedicated to Ken in those days of youth. I know I was in denial about it all. He treated me like shit most of the time. He was very controlling of what I did and whom I did it with. I fell for it though. I thought maybe I wouldn't find anyone else; that I had to figure out a way to make this work. I felt that good and bad were a part of life, which is such bullshit if you were to ask me now. Yet, I kept it going long after I returned to Paw Paw, Michigan; putting my life on hold while I took care of his.

Ken was not supportive of anything with me. He was mean verbally and would call me all sorts of names. I found out so much living with him, the real deal I guess. I am sure I had my moments, but I was no match for Ken, Ken being 6'5"; he was a big guy with a violent side. I couldn't seem to do anything right. He really just wanted another wife to cook and clean, which again just wasn't my thing although I did try. He didn't want me to ever shower without him and if I did he would get really pissed. One night I made spaghetti. I served him the meal and sat down. He got up, went across the room, threw the entire plate at me and said it was horrible and overcooked. With Ken I just clammed up. I would just sit still, let him go off on me and say nothing. Not for long, though.

I didn't have many friends with Ken. He was very controlling of my friends and wouldn't let me hang out with them. One time I was on the phone with Lynn and he kept screaming, "Who is it!?" I finally screamed back, "It's Lynn," and he hauled off and punched me in the stomach. My Dad didn't like Ken at all. As a matter of fact he hated the thought of his little girl even shacking up with a man at such a young age. I was 21 at this point. I turned the big 21 in Detroit; the legal drinking age. Anyway, if my mom and dad came by to visit, Dad would never come inside. My mom would for a minute but not Dad. Mom of course kept her opinions to herself, she never showed it, but I am sure she didn't care for Ken either. She put up with it just to see me.

Chapter Five

Ken was working the third shift at the factory and I was fresh back from Detroit. My first job in Radio was at this small mom and pop station in Hastings. I didn't stay long before I was offered a job at another radio station in Kalamazoo. I had been depressed with my life. Work was the only thing that offered me joy. Ken always cut me down, saying I wasn't any good at anything I did. I was asked to sing for my mom's friend's daughter's wedding and I was so excited about singing again. Ken wouldn't go with me because he said I sucked and didn't want any part of what I was doing. I ended up singing at the ceremony and did a great job, vocally. I forgot some of the words and made it up as I went along. I was so nervous since I hadn't performed in a while. When I was younger, I was on stage all the time singing and dancing, doing musicals. The stage was my passion and I was good at it. As I got older, though, I stopped performing because I needed to make a living and doing free shows just wouldn't pay the bills. Although entertaining has always been in my blood, my life took a different path. Now, when I feel inspired I just head out for a night of karaoke.

Sex with Ken was all about Ken. I am pretty sure I faked every single
orgasm. I was so afraid half of the time that I wasn't pleasing him, so I
would invent ways to make the sex interesting. He was happy just getting
on top and going for the ride. He thought that because he had a big penis
that was all he needed to keep me happy. All these years later and I can't
even remember if he did have a big penis. I know he told me I would
never find another guy to satisfy me like he did since he had the biggest
penis in the world. I guess it's all relative. I just can't recall. So one night
I wanted to have some fun and I kept pestering him about role-playing. I
had bugged him before about this and he always pushed it off. Tonight he
decided to take it to the limit. I was the queen of the castle and Ken had to
kidnap me… on and on I went until finally he grabbed me and threw me to
the ground. He had rope and a gag stashed under the couch. He tied me up,
gagged me and carried me to the back room. Ken had an old weight bench
that he never used. He stripped me down, bent me over and tied my hands
to the bottom. I was bent over the back of the bench and he proceeded to
rape me. He left the room and came back with some vibrators; he then
raped me over and over again with the toys. He kept saying, "You want it
so bad? You got it, bitch." It was the real thing, no role-playing here. I was
crying pretty hard by now, begging him to let me go. He left the room and

56

left me there for what seemed to be hours. I just hung there crying and begging for him to let me go. I can't remember how this ended; I can imagine it wasn't good when he finally released me.

Life went on like this for a while. I was still doing coke and meth pretty heavy and he was smoking pot until it poured out of his ass. If he was high he was easier to deal with, but sober, forget it. I took a part time job at a bar in Paw Paw. I was a waitress; I actually liked this job. I got great tips so I could party more. I met a guy, John here. He was so incredibly good looking. I felt honored he even had an interest in me. Every time he came in we flirted like crazy and finally we took it to a new level. This would be the first guy I cheated on Ken with, and yes it was worth it. When I look back I actually wish I had dumped Ken's sorry ass and went for John. John and I had a great connection but he grew tired of me not getting rid of Ken. I don't know; maybe I was scared, scared of what he would do. I can remember one big fight and for no reason, really. I can remember how Ken beat the shit out of me and threw me all over the trailer. He threw all of my jewelry out, trashed my things, and then he threw me out the door. It was early in the morning when he got off work. I was crashed on the couch when he came in and went off. I had this tiny see-through top on, and he just threw me out and locked the door. At this point I was really at the end of my rope with the relationship and started thinking of a way out. I finally got one.

I was given a better job. I now worked for a top 40 station and I was much more into this. It was still part time, but it was a great gig and I liked it. I was visiting with mom and dad when I got a phone call from the past. Linda was in town. Linda was forced into getting married when she was 15 and had been living in Alabama for years. I hadn't heard from her in a long time and when she called I was dying to see my old friend. She was in Michigan to buy a car and then she would return to Alabama. Once she and I hooked up, all hell broke loose. She, too, had been into meth, coke and pot pretty heavily like myself, so we had that in common. She also had some connections, so I was dealing the meth and storing it in the back of the trailer. Ken hated Linda and knew we were up to no good together. He couldn't stop me this time.

Linda ended up fucking Ken's cousin at our trailer and his wife busted them. Before long, word got back to Linda's husband and they ended up in divorce. I had the IRS on my ass for not paying taxes on un-employment. I just didn't get that... I had no idea that I had to pay taxes on money the government was giving to me because I had no money. How was I to pay taxes when I had no money? That's why I was on un-employment! The whole system is fucked up, to me. It makes no sense at all. I had no choice; I had to pay the bill. Fear, that's all that was, and because I was ignorant I fell for it.

I was working at the radio station and hanging out with Linda. We were becoming inseparable. Life with Ken was unbearable and I started making plans for my escape. A good friend from high school was diagnosed with cancer a few years back. He had bone cancer and he and I had remained friends through all of this. Because I was pretty heavy into drugs, I started to move myself away from people that didn't approve of my drug use. He was one of them. He was always such a great friend, but my mind was clouded due to no sleep, no food and endless nights of partying.

I finally got up the courage to leave Ken. It was during the night when he was working third shift. I packed up what I could and moved into another trailer with Linda. Her mom had this place and let us live in it for a while. This was a pretty nice trailer on a great piece of property. To pick up some extra cash, I decided to start DJing on the side. I mostly did weddings before Linda came around, and when she came back and couldn't get a job I brought her in on the gigs. She was terrible at it, but the company was just fine with me, and since Linda and I couldn't do anything without each other the company was fine with us. When we moved in together we decided to start a business. I did some marketing and we started DJing for ladies night at the Crystal Club (how ironic). We called ourselves the "Jamming Jockettes" and boy did we draw in the male crowd.

Most of the woman hated us, but we didn't give a shit. It was business and we were really good at it. I was booking weddings like crazy and we had some pretty sweet equipment; I did anyway.

We went to my dad for business advice and he tried to encourage me to not venture into business with Linda; I did anyway. We had this guy that we were buying and selling coke for, he was into it big time. One night he came by and dumped a shit load of coke on the round glass table I had. The line reached from one side of the table to the other and yes, I snorted it, taking a break half way through the line. This guy had us sign all this paperwork and we borrowed a good amount of money from him to get more equipment. This was all good until we decided not to pay him back. Shit, we were planning a way to break into his house and steal his stash and his cash. Not a good idea! One night when Linda and I were sitting at home all coked up a guy pulled into the driveway, got out of his car and pulled a couple rounds off; just as a warning to pay our bill.

I decided this was no guy to mess with and I tried to talk with him, to no avail. He wanted his money. So we just got deeper and deeper into this shit. Now we were selling the coke all cut with baby laxative to make more money. We would keep the uncut version for ourselves of course. This went on for a long time before people started talking about our shit, cut up drugs and the sales started to decline.

Linda wasn't really bringing in much cash. She did this odd job working car detailing. I was working at the station one night and let me tell you things were pretty crazy in Radio, back in the days when I could smoke while being on the air. I was having no problems at all with guys wanting to hook up with me. There was no shortage of them at all. I was just about to go on the air when a fellow DJ who was standing next to me said, "I bet I can masturbate myself in the trash can in the time it takes for you to open and close the mic." I am thinking no way, but sure enough I turn on the mic and he drops his pants and starts to masturbate. Before I turn the mic off he has cum all over the trashcan! Ah, the good old radio days! One night Linda and I decided to invite this guy from the station over for a little ménage à trois. He was more than excited to have a three some with the Jammin Jockettes. Linda and I were fucking around with everyone and anyone, although we had our favorites that kept coming back. My favorite was this guy I met in a band and Linda's was another guy from that band. We met these guys at a bar when they were playing. My guy was the lead singer and keyboard player. This guy was married but had no problem finding time for me. I actually think that he preferred me, but he had kids and didn't want to go through a divorce. He would be the first guy to give me a real orgasm (no faking it)! I remember being with him at this house and he went down on me. He talked to me and really took the time to get me to relax and enjoy the experience. Boy, did I do that and twice. I never had an orgasm before, and now twice! So you can see how I confused this experience with love. To think I had gone so long faking it. Boy, had I been missing out.

Linda and I loved the fact that these guys were friends and we all got together. We did our thing for quite a while, but at some point he got really possessive and didn't want me seeing other guys. Here he is married! I didn't care for this too much but I didn't want to give up the good sex either. One night when Linda and I were working at the club his wife decided to show up and confront me. I was so cocky at this time that it didn't even bother me. Bring it on bitch! I knew I could take her on, but that got broke up pretty fast. Years later this guy called me (I was getting married at this time) and he was finally going to get a divorce. He was afraid her attorney would contact me and have me go to court to talk about his cheating days. He wanted custody of the kids. Good thing that never happened because I wouldn't have lied.

I left the radio station I was at to take a full time gig at another station. I hated this station but I really needed a full time job. The station did oldies, sports, news and all of that boring crap. I did sports for a while but was dropped from that because I couldn't pronounce half of the player's names correctly. My boss at the station was a total ass. I'm not sure why he hired me; he never liked me. I ran most of the shows on the weekends. All I had to do was show up, change out reels and talk once in a while. Sundays were the worst; they played a bunch of religious shows. I would put the reel on and go take a nap in the bathroom. One time my alarm didn't go off and I still have no idea how long I had dead air. I got busted a few times for this but nothing ever happened. Then, one Sunday Linda and I came in together after being up all night. We just sat talking and we kept snorting coke to keep going. I had to change out a reel and announce the next one. It was Easter Sunday and I open the mic and say, "this is the day that Jesus Christ had an erection." Linda went off in hysterics and I just kept going. I never saw that board light up with so many callers. My boss never heard that one; I'm sure I would have been fired if he did.

It's now time for Linda and I to head back to Alabama and pick up the leftovers from her marriage. Once we got there she broke into her old home and stole a bunch of business checks; she couldn't find anything else of value. We got ourselves a hotel room and hooked up with some of her drug dealer friends. It was strange; I liked the way it felt to be around these rich guys, having all the drugs I wanted and hanging out by the pool all day. The guy actually offered for Linda and I to be mules. He thought we could easily carry drugs by plane. No one would mess with two good-looking girls. Needless to say, we declined. Our last night in Alabama the guys came over to do some free basing, which was something I hadn't tried before and didn't plan on starting. Linda and I both declined, the guys did their thing, and we passed out. They left, we missed our flight, and I was put on probation at work. I ended up going into the bank to cash a check that Linda had stolen. She didn't have an account, so I had to cash it. She wrote the check for three thousand dollars. I was so nervous about doing this that I forgot to sign the back of the check; they never noticed. They cashed it, we spent it and then they called saying the account had been closed and they wanted their money back. They called for a long time, but since I never signed the back they were kind of shit out of luck. I guess they ended up writing it off. Another money nightmare came when Linda was working at this auto detailing place and she stole checks from a girl's car. We decided to see how many we could use before it got too risky. We got away with a few at the gas station, but then the word was out and we ended up getting on camera. I can't remember how this all played out; I do know that the cops were calling endlessly, but for some reason they couldn't do a thing about it.

Tonight I made the move that I thought never would happen, but 5 years later, I moved all my stuff out of Ken's. I do miss him, I miss the security, I miss my future being all set. Now I'm starting over and it's not a good start so far! I've gotten into a little shit and I'm confused half the time. I'm so drugged, I don't even face reality, but when I come down it hits and it's hard. I need to get the hell out of this town, this state! I really am losing it ya know and I don't know where to turn.

(no date)

Losing it, HA! I'm going fucking crazy! I'm so very lonely I could die. Die, now that's a word I think about often! How easy it would be! I pull myself out of the hole and fall back again and again. I can't handle it!

I met up with this chick in Lawton, Michigan. I can't remember how I met her, but I remember her well. She was pretty fucked up herself. Linda was spending all her time with a new guy, and I needed someone to hang with. This chick and I hit it off; we sat around and snorted coke all day long. If I supplied her with downers she would keep my nose full. Her shit was good too and I was very addicted at this time. I did a lot of dealing with her until one night when my friend was on his deathbed. I went to him; first, though, I should say seeing him in this condition was so painful. He was living back with his parents in Mattawan where they had him in the living room lying in a hospital bed with machines all hooked up. The cancer had spread and he was beyond help or remission at this point. He at one point did the chemo but hated it. He decided when it's time to go, it's time to go. At least he would be going out looking good. He had beautiful lush black hair, deep brown eyes and a handsome smile. He wasn't smiling today. Often his mom would stay in the room but I did get some time alone with him. He looked so small in this big bed, his body had reduced to almost nothing and the life was going out of his eyes. I told him some lie about wanting some pain pills and he told me to go over to the counter where he had bottles and bottles of pain pills. He was kind enough to give me some. He never asked too many questions; all he said was that he didn't need them anymore. I took those pain pills over to that girl's house and we would exchange. She got wind of this situation and talked me into going back for some more. You see, I didn't have any emotions at this time; I was a zombie, and all I wanted was more. I have never told this story before; it took me many years to come to terms with. I have no regrets for what happened, it happened just as it did. I find no reason to live in the past with regrets that only weigh you down. You just have to look at your behavior and own it, and then you can let it go. So this girl and I make a plan to go over to my friends, and while I am stealing pain pills she will distract the mom. I was terrified of being caught but she held up her end of the bargain and kept the mom in the kitchen. My friend was so out of it. I tried to talk with him and he kept dozing off. So, I found my window and I crawled through. I dumped hundreds of those pain pills in my purse, some from every bottle that said "may cause drowsiness." At one point, when I was putting the bottle back, I took a glance over at him and I will never forget the look on his face. He had his head propped up and he had been watching me. I immediately looked away in shame and left. That was the last time I saw him alive.

I got the news that my friend had died one day when I was at my parents. I still had no tears. I just ran away. Linda and I went to his funeral, which was overflowing with people who had loved him as I did; still no tears. It was some time later before I finally broke down. I was driving into work and had been dry for a few days when it just hit me. I lost it; everything I had bottled up came pouring out. Everything! I stayed clean for a while, but only for a while.

Chapter Six

Linda and I decided to move out of the trailer and get a place in Lawrence. Her mom ended up moving in with us and that was cramping our style. We got this place way out in nowhere land, a tiny little dump that has those bugs called "earwigs". They were everywhere: on the ceiling, on the walls, under the tables. A few bites told me not to mess around and just kill the bastards. I had once again changed jobs and now was working for a classic rock radio station. I really liked this job. I worked nights and started doing commercial scripting. I loved writing and producing commercials and I enjoyed being on the air. I had my share of followers too; one night this guy brought me dinner. When he left and I opened the container I just about gagged. It had dog hair all over it. This wasn't intentional; he really was doing something nice, it was just how he lived. I had to throw it out! Linda and I started dating these two brothers that we went to high school with, once again I got the older one. Ron was way better looking. We started hanging out with them all of the time. Ron was an Ok guy. Both brothers still lived with mommy and daddy, which was annoying, so they would hang at our place most of the time. One night Ron told me I could be a ten if I just lost a few pounds. Hanging out at their parent's house one night (which turned into 3 or 4 since his parents were away) we took the three wheelers out back for some fun cornfield riding. I was driving first and Ron was on the back. We started to get some speed and the race began. Ron couldn't stand that I was driving so he decided to climb over me and push me back while we were flying through the corn. No sooner had he gotten in position than he hit the throttle and we were slamming through the corn. I didn't get a chance to lift my legs up and the corn got hold of them, slapping and snapping. It all went so fast, within seconds both my legs were dragged up under the tires and my shoes and socks were ripped right off of my feet. I screamed and screamed but Ron kept going until I dug my nails so deep into his neck he had no choice but to stop. It was pretty bad. My legs were torn down to the bones and I couldn't feel anything. They got me back to the house and Linda put me in the tub, cleaned my wounds and brought me a bottle of tequila. I drank the pain away, but come morning I was in so much pain that I thought I would die. I stayed at Ron's for a couple of days; he felt so guilty he just wanted to take care of me. The station was sponsoring an air show and I really wanted to go, so I put the pain behind me and went. As the day went on my foot got bigger and bigger; it was full of puss. I ended up going to the hospital and, to make a long story short, they gave me the wrong pills and my foot got worse. It got so bad they talked about amputation. That never happened, they figured it out and everything worked out. I was so pissed at Ron for his ego play that I dumped his ass.

Linda and I were still chumming, doing the bar thing, tripping on acid, the whole lot. We met tons of people doing the DJ thing at the bar and when we weren't working there we were partying there. The owner of the bar (or his son) had the hots for me, so I pretty much got whatever I wanted. I played him and he didn't seem to mind. Chad was a cool dude we met at the club. Linda really wanted him and I really wasn't to attracted to Chad. Chad and I were buds and Chad and Linda were lovers. After the bar closed one night, Chad let Linda take his truck. We wanted to run to Oshtemo to get a burger. It was in the winter and we had just had a pretty good snowstorm. The roads were icy though they had cleared up a bit. This was Chad's brand new truck and here we went, off for our late night fix. Linda was driving and we were heading down Red Arrow Highway. Just as we were going around this curve, we hit a patch of ice. All I remember is "hold on we are going to hit that hill" (we didn't have seatbelts on). I remember actually having a discussion on what we would hit and then lights out! There was a car behind us that watched the whole thing. When I came to, Linda was screaming. We were upside down and we both frantically crawled out of the broken window. These girls from the other car were screaming and running towards us. I guess we rolled about 4 times (I think) down the road. We hit a bank and it flipped us until we came to a halt, upside down. My head was bleeding pretty badly, a house near the accident heard it all and the people living there came running out. They called an ambulance, and since I was messed up pretty bad the paramedics hauled my ass off. My brother was a paramedic at this time and had one of those radios in our parents' house. I kept saying that Wilson was my brother, hoping we wouldn't get into trouble. My parents heard the report on the radio and headed off to the hospital. I know that Linda never got in trouble even though she was driving, but we totaled Chad's brand new truck. My Dad walked into the hospital room and said, "It smells like a god damn brewery." Then he walked off. I'm sure it did smell like a brewery. I got a ton of staples in my head and then I was sent home. Linda and I swore this was life changing; maybe it was for a moment, but then we were back to our old selves again.

Things were getting pretty desperate. We never had enough money and I started to get really tired of the whole scene. Chad and I hooked up for a while; he said it was always me he wanted to be with. Linda never knew about this. I was discreet but I couldn't say that about her. If she wanted to fuck a guy I was with she would just do it and I would walk in on it. We weren't too loyal to the guys or to each other.

The Crystal Club is where I met Andy, my first husband. He was such a doll but also a rebel, I liked that. He was actually younger than me. Maybe I was just tired of the whole game, I was feeling that it was time to get some stability. I don't really know. I know I was tired of Linda and I needed to get my life in order. I had dreams but Linda had none; I knew if I kept going it wasn't going to get better but worse. I just didn't want to end up like that, a waste. Andy and I really hit it off. We started spending all of our time together. I think he loved me for how he knew love; I really don't know, we were young. Linda started hooking up with Aaron, Andy's brother and I felt like she was just using him to be close to me. I decided to share with Aaron that Linda was out fucking Charlie while she shacked up with him. Linda and I both left our apartment and moved in with Aaron and Andy. It was Aaron's house. Slowly, things with Linda got really ugly so Andy and I thought it best to move in with my parents. Before I left, Linda and I had it out pretty good. I was never afraid of Linda, I felt pretty sure I could kick her ass if it came to that. Once we moved out, Linda and I pretty much ended our relationship. She latched on to Aaron and I latched on to Andy. Aaron had three kids from another marriage and the kids were pretty young at this time. I heard that Aaron and Linda packed up the truck, left everything behind and went to Phoenix for a while. Next, I heard they were living in the South somewhere and that Linda was pretty hooked on downers. I never wanted to hear the gossip about how fucked up Aaron and Linda were, but people love to share what they know. I also heard that Aaron woke up one night and found Linda sucking on Chris's dick. Chris is Aaron's son; he was 12. The rumor is that she had been teaching Chris all about sex, and that they had been having sex for quite a while. This time they got caught. I guess Aaron put a gun to Linda's head and threatened to kill her. This is all a rumor, but honestly nothing surprises me about what Linda would do. She and I have never spoken again nor have I seen her.

Mom and Dad weren't too thrilled about Andy and I moving into their house. Dad was more so than Mom. Dad would say, "What kind of a guy shacks up with his girlfriend's parents?" It was a struggle living with my parents and we knew if we wanted to stay together that we needed our own place. My dad's parents had passed away and they had a trailer sitting around that we ended up moving into. It was weird but we did it, we needed to. Andy had proposed to me out on Lake Michigan. He even got down on one knee and presented the ring. He arranged a nice dinner on a boat. I never did cry, I guess I thought it was time; it was the thing to do. I did love him, right? Later I was told that not crying was a sign to run fast and far. I just wasn't much of a public crier, or a crier at all. I didn't really show that emotion that much. I accepted the proposal and we set the date for May 22, 1992. Everyone seemed to be quite happy about the whole thing, his family and my family. So plans were set in motion. Being I was the only girl, I knew my mom would love making all the plans. I really didn't care too much. Being in the wedding business, I pretty much knew what I wanted and I got it.

It was a big tripped out wedding. Aaron and Linda weren't invited but the rest of the world was. Shit, my Mom invited people I didn't even know. I didn't care though, more money for us to start our new lives; and besides, we weren't paying for it. Both sides pretty much paid for what they were "responsible" for. Who makes up those rules anyway? Over 300 people showed. I had the huge puffy dress, Andy had this weird puffy hair do; a mullet is what they called it. Right before I walked down the aisle, I turned to my dad and said, "I don't want to do this." He said, "It's a little too late, don't cha think?" I must have agreed because I made it down the aisle. I sang to my husband to be, said "I do" and walked out. Signed, sealed and delivered! This part of the book won't be long, since the marriage didn't even last a year. That night we danced and snorted it up all night long, then hopped on a plane for Jamaica.

Chapter Seven

We got a hold of some kick ass pot in Jamaica. Andy got really sick and I got my hair braided. Hm... what else? Nothing really, the honeymoon wasn't that great! Life went on. I kept doing the powder and Andy did his share as well. We had our parties, our dogs, and our so-called married life. I just couldn't get into the domestic thing. I tried, I did, and it just wasn't me. Andy made me promise him that I would push out at least one kid. Having kids was something I never wanted to do and here I was making a promise that I knew I couldn't keep. Since Andy had gotten married, he was being responsible and getting respected more at work. He was promoted to foreman, or something like that. He had worked third shift at a plastics company for a long time and now he would be doing the morning shift. We found this cute little house in Otsego. We didn't have a lot of money so Dad lent us the down payment. Here I am, 25, owning a house with two dogs and married with no children. I had left radio and took a job with cable. I was finally a producer; I really loved this job writing and producing television commercials. Our company moved from Battle Creek to Grand Rapids and I commuted a good hour drive every day. I really can't remember how it all came to an end. Andy and I were becoming so distant from each other. We never really saw each other once he was back on third shift. I was really into my work and not really into being a wife. We went on a one-year anniversary to Las Vegas, which was a joke! We fought the entire time and even talked about divorce. I remember coming home from work for lunch one day and he was not home. Andy started going to the bar after work and not coming home until really late, then he would just sleep all night until he had to be back at work. The marriage was just falling apart, I knew it, I just didn't know why? One morning I woke up to a letter from Andy saying he didn't love me anymore and wanted a divorce, he would be gone for a while and P.S. please feed the dogs! I was so upset I went on a rampage and destroyed everything that had anything to do with him. Mary came over; we made a huge pile of Andy's stuff in the driveway and set it on fire! I knew it was over, I knew there was no talking, no nothing. It was done and it was time for me to move on. He came home and we got into a heated argument where he proceeded to tell me I would make a terrible mother to his children because I didn't chew gum? Yeah, I didn't get that one either. The house was mine, yet I knew I didn't want that kind of stability. I wanted to leave; I didn't want to keep anything. While we were married I had started DJing again on the weekends for extra income and I was stashing that into an account. Andy would come along once in a while, but we fought way too much about who was getting hit on. It was either he or I getting hit on and we were just way too insecure to work through the jealousy. I recall doing Andy's Christmas party very well. He even helped me set up and worked the gig with me. I will never forget this girl with long black hair that kept walking by the table and making eyes at Andy. I knew then that he was cheating on me. That truth didn't come out for a while, though it eventually did, and I was still in denial. I really never thought for a moment that he would cheat on me. I must have had that fear, yet felt he loved me too much to ever do that. Anyway, all of my friends came to my rescue and helped me move out and into my parents' old house on the lake, which was vacant at this time. Man, did we trash Andy's place, I took everything that I felt was mine. I really didn't want anything, I just wanted out and wanted to start anew. Andy had drained my account and left me with five dollars, so I went to a lawyer and the cost for him was not worth the fight. So I just let it go. Andy got the bikes, the furniture, the bed… he really got it all. He got the house; I sold him the house and then had to split the profit with him, which was only five hundred dollars.

Tim put a tuna fish sandwich up in the ceiling, Mary cut all the buttons off of his shirts and put an earring in the waterbed (yes, the bed did end up leaking), and I put cards and photos all over the place to remind him of what we once had. Right before we shut the door, we hiked up the heater to as far as it would go! Did any of this make me feel better? No, but it wasn't about that.

Time went by living out on the lake. Andy would call now and then to beg for me to come back. I ended up hearing through friends that Andy had been cheating on me from the beginning and in that he got that girl, the one I saw at the party, pregnant. I knew I would never go back to him, but his cheating really hurt; it took years for me to come to some sort of peace with it. In the meantime I was a loose canon and could care less. I was still doing coke big time with Andy's friends. I had to break the ties I had, I was tired of hearing about him. A friend once told me that a true sign of a guy cheating on you is that he will blame you for cheating on him. This made sense. I remember Linda cheated on her husband and she would always tell me how paranoid she was of him cheating on her; how she use to smell his underwear. Andy always accused me of cheating on him and I never did. One morning, I woke up to him accusing me of being out with a guy and that I had to have just gotten home because he felt the hood of the car and he swore it was still hot. He rummaged through my purse and found a piece of paper with a guys name on it. It was the name of a guy who I was going to call to build a deck for the backyard. So, it's true that what you fear the most will eventually come to fruition. I was downstairs during one of Andy's and my parties snorting some coke with a friend of his when he burst in, accusing us of fooling around. This friend of his was a cheat, but not with me. That night I got up, snuck around the house and peaked in the front window to find Andy's friend getting it on with Mary; his wife was downstairs sleeping. Once Andy and I had decided to separate, he was sleeping downstairs and I slept upstairs. We never spoke to each other; we just went on existing until I could move out. One night after work I went out with some co-workers. My boss and I were having a good time together and we got pretty fucked up. I went back to his house so I wouldn't have to drive. He and I ended up having sex; it was pretty good. I felt so guilty about this since Andy and I weren't divorced just yet. I didn't come home until the next morning and was really hung over. I got home and Andy actually wanted to talk. He was actually wondering if we should stay together, but at this point I knew it was over. I could never forgive myself for sleeping with Scott when I was still married and I couldn't lie to Andy and expect him to forgive me. I didn't know at this time that he had already been sleeping around. I suspected but I didn't know for sure. I just started an argument with him to get him to realize that it was done; there was no turning back.

I can't deny that I was depressed and lonely all of the time and was trying to fill that void with different men, drugs and alcohol. They didn't work, but I tried. I started hanging out with Tim and Lynn. When I left Andy I needed to find someone to help me with the DJing, so I brought on Lynn. Then Tim had to get in on it as well. We started booking many bar gigs, which of course led to more partying and more men. So many men, I stopped counting at this point. Tim was pretty attached to me, trying to be my protector. He was working for a furniture store at this time. One day Lynn and I went in to see him and this is where I met Jim. Jim was quite a few years older than me, but we hit it off right away and I really wanted to go out with him. Tim kept trying to persuade me not to, saying that Jim being his boss and all it wasn't a good idea. He introduced me to his other friend Ken who was also a part-time cop. Knowing I had left everything behind, they felt compelled to get me some furniture. I was getting all sorts of cool new stuff. I got a new bed, new lamps, a table and chairs, side dressers and more and more. It just kept coming. One day I came home to find more furniture in my house and also that this Ken guy had broken in to drop it off (along with a nice cum stain on the bed to show he was there). I was starting to get really creeped out by this Ken guy; he just wouldn't go away. Then I came to find out he was married. I tried to put an end to it and he just kept harassing me. Tim wouldn't do anything about it. I wanted to know where all this furniture was coming from too; I just didn't like what was going on. At some point Ken just gave up on me and went away.

It took a good year for the divorce with Andy to be final. My Dad had said that the money he gave to Andy and myself was a gift, and since the marriage didn't last he wanted his money back. He loaned us $5,000. I didn't have that kind of money laying around and when I asked Andy if he would give me half to pay my dad back he said "no way." For a really long time my Dad wouldn't even talk to me. I kept trying to talk to him about the pain of the divorce and tell him that I would do what I could to get him some money; he just wouldn't hear it! After I had moved to Grand Rapids and saved up some money, I called to have my parents up for a visit. Dad and I went for a drive. It was during Christmas and he wasn't saying much. We stopped and picked out a tree for my apartment. I started crying and telling him how I was devastated by what Andy did and blah, blah, blah. Dad could care less, he says he has endured many things and you just don't talk about it. "It's in the past." He didn't want to hear any excuses; he just wanted his five thousand dollars. I told him I had $500 and that was the best I could do. He took the money and said we would never talk about it again. We haven't.

Life was pretty crazy for quite a while living in Grand Rapids, being single. For the 1994 New Year, Lynn, Tim and I got a limo, went out bar hopping all night and stayed in a pretty high-end hotel. Tim pretty much passed out at a certain point but Lynn and I weren't done just yet. We went down to the pool but it was closed, so we found a guy that was working and begged him to let us swim. In return we would meet him in a room and give him a good time. We did just that: gave this guy a time I'm sure he hasn't forgotten today. Tim never knew a thing.

All three of us decided to do a fun trip to Florida, so we packed up the van and headed out. My brother Robert had been living there for quite a while now. We got this dump hotel in Fort Lauderdale and boy did we party. I was so fucked up most of the time I can't remember most of the trip. I do remember taking a boat over to the Bahamas and parasailing for the first time, that was incredible. I also remember partying at the bar Giggles with Robert. Robert introduced me to this guy he worked for, his name was Robert. I ended up going home with him, fucking him and regretting that come morning. Looks do change when you're drunk. I got out of that, yet he took a liking to me , which actually comes in handy for me later down the road.

I finally got together with Jim from the furniture store and we dated for quite a while. I was still working at cable, living in Grand Rapids, DJing and just doing. I had made some great friends at cable and was still pretty dedicated to my future in broadcast. My friend Mary decided that I needed a man who would never shit on me, so she got me a kitty. I named him Schekki. He was so damn cute. I couldn't resist, although I really didn't want the responsibilities of taking care of a cat. Schekki is black and white, and when you put his two front paws together it makes the shape of a heart. He is my heart, I love this cat, and I still have him today.

Jim was a bit of a challenge for a boyfriend. He worked all the time and when he said he would come over, he would get caught up in something else and never show up. He has two girls, one was ten and one was thirteen. I never ever liked dating guys with kids, but his kids seemed to like me and they weren't babies so I could deal with it. He and his ex-wife shared custody, so the kids weren't always with him. Those girls were spoiled rotten. Jim was pretty wealthy, at least what I considered wealthy. He told me at one point he was making about $250 thousand. He was a tight ass though. He never bought me anything, he never wanted to meet my parents and he lied about his age. His ex was a maniac and I grew very tired of her drama. She would call at all hours of the night, hating that I was with Jim. Jim had the smallest dick I had ever seen or felt. The sex was not good at all, I could never feel him inside of me and sucking him was a joke! The oral sex just wasn't happening either. You ask, what was my interest? It had to have been the money; I'm really not sure. Maybe it was the thought of some kind of secure relationship? It doesn't matter because it didn't last that long.

One day at my apartment Jim asked where I got all this furniture. At this time I knew something was up and I didn't know what to say. He checked his computer and found that I had only bought two things from them, and now was demanding to know where it came from. I told him and that of course turned into a huge nightmare. First, that I would even accept the stuff pissed Jim off and then Tim was pissed at me for telling. Both Ken and Tim were fired. It was a big deal. They were sued and their homes were checked. Sure enough they found all kinds of stolen furniture. All of that had to be returned. I gladly let them come and take the stuff away and decided to just buy my own. I wanted to believe that the furniture wasn't stolen. I knew, I just didn't want to admit it.

Life was becoming a blur. Jim and I broke it off and I was on the prowl again. One night I was out doing it up. I can't even remember half of the people that I have partied with but I was with these people and had been snorting a lot of coke and drinking. They had invited this guy over that they wanted to hook me up with. He was a dog, flat out ugly and I was so pissed off that they thought I would have any interest in this loser. I left and went home. I was pretty wired from the coke and needed to come down, so I smoked some pot and that didn't help much. I was listening to Wilson Philips and feeling pretty down on myself.

I called Mary and told her I was tired and wanted to kill myself. She basically said, "Grow up and go to bed." That was it for me; I swallowed a whole bottle of Xanax then called 911. When they answered I hung up the phone and they called right back. Next thing I knew the house was full of cops and paramedics. I was pretty much out of it, yet I remember one guy saying, "Why would you do this?" I said, "because of men," and he said "You would kill yourself over men?" I also remember making a statement that this was the first time I ever had so many men in my house and I was too fucked up to do anything. Pretty sad, huh? I was sad; I passed out and woke up in the hospital. My parents were there and so was Mary. I ended up staying at my parents' house for a few days; Mary picked up Schekki and brought him there. My parents never talked to me about it, it was dropped like everything else.

Chapter Eight

I needed to get away for a while and do some soul searching, so I booked a Club Med trip to Mexico. This was a great female bonding trip although I did meet this guy that really impressed me. He spoke five different languages and was really good in bed. We had our little Mexico fling. He was married but we managed to keep in touch after I came home. We met up one time in Michigan for a one nighter then he was off and I never saw him again. He called at one point and accused me of giving him warts. I'm sure he was sleeping with other women neither his wife nor I knew about. What I did know was that I didn't give him warts! Vacations always end and you're back doing what you are doing, the same old shit. Work, drink, drugs, men, and maybe sleep depending on how wired I was.

I was starting to get tired of cable, almost 6 years at the same gig and things were starting to get pretty Nazi like there. I knew I needed to take what I had learned and get out. I flew to Colorado for an interview, but that never panned out. Back to Grand Rapids, back to cable.

I had an early morning shoot with another producer, Dave, and I alsoneeded to get back in time for an interview I had set up with a country radio station. For extra income I was also doing part time radio and they approached me for a morning show position. I always wanted to do mornings and I ran to this opportunity. Dave dropped me off at the apartment and asked to come in to use the bathroom. He knew I had to change for the interview and as I was in the bedroom, I heard the shower running. I knocked on the door and he had decided to jump in the shower! I went back in the bedroom, got dressed and when I came out he was sitting on the couch naked. I turned my back and said "Dave put your clothes on." He said, "I will show you mine if you show me yours." I just about died! I'm so sure; I have an interview, get the fuck out! I was sexually harassed all the time at cable. It really was no big deal to me since it gave me some attention, and it never went any further unless I wanted it to. My boss was always making sexual comments and I would just laugh it off!

Laughing it off is what I did most of the time when things weren't going so great. I left cable and took the morning job in radio. I was nothing more then a sidekick, they brought in this high dollar guy from Texas to run the show. AJ and I were his little puppets. We made the show and he made all of the money. I was basically being paid to laugh at this guy's stupid jokes. My pay was the most I had ever made, $30,000 a year! When I worked at cable I became friends with a great guy, Eddie. He and I became really close. We went out all the time to pick up strange and if we didn't get any we always had each other. He was my bar buddy and friend. I remember meeting this one guy, Shawn. I was pretty fucked up and Shawn talked me into taking a ride with him. I ended up way up north in a hotel the next morning with him on top of me trying to dry hump me. I pushed him off and just wanted to get the fuck out of there. Well, it was a good five hours back home and I knew I had to figure a way out without pissing him off. I was so drunk the night before I didn't really notice that he was a bit off, strange, I can't really describe it. I just wanted to go home. I faked being really sick as he drove me home. I got out and never saw him again. He called and bugged me for a while, but eventually gave up! I had many fucked up nights like this, some really close calls. Yet I somehow survived it.

I ended up losing my job at the station; we were just not hitting our numbers. They let us all go except for the main guy, mainly because they had a contract with him and they had no choice. I decided it was time to get out of Grand Rapids, time to go somewhere fresh, so I made all of the arrangements to move to Fort Lauderdale, Florida. I mentioned Robert earlier, the guy I met in Florida. Well I needed a place to stay and I thought of him. I figured I could crash at his place until I found a place of my own. He wasn't too excited about the idea but agreed to it anyway. He had that wild Italian energy, really loud and obnoxious. I knew I wouldn't be able to take that for too long. Eddie helped me move, we packed up a trailer and my 4-Runner and off we went to Florida. We met my parents for breakfast before we went and this was the second time I saw my dad cry. Eddie drove, he actually did all of the driving, and when he dropped me off he stayed a couple days then flew home. The last thing he said to me was, "Get the hell outta there!" Oh yeah, I knew what he was talking about; Robert was a whack case! I had no job, no money, and I needed to find a place and soon.

I can't remember how long it took before I found an apartment. Robert got really strange, really possessive. He tried like hell to get me to sleep with him, threatening me, yet I kept saying no and tried to keep my distance. He hated Schekki. One morning I woke up to find that Robert had thrown him outside and I found him under a bush crying. He was such an asshole. He never said I had to pay rent, but when he found out I wouldn't fuck him he decided to make me pay. I didn't have a job yet, I was out everyday looking for whatever I could get, nothing! Robert was a big time pot dealer, a major stoner. I knew I had to get out. After all of the mental bullshit, I finally found a place and got the hell out. He hounded me for quite a while, coming over and banging on my door demanding money. I couldn't pay him. I was broke! He did threaten my life and I taped the messages that he left on my machine. He was one crazy motherfucker. Eventually he gave up on me and that was fine, yet I always felt like I was looking over my shoulder.

The new apartment was nice; I finally got a job at a talent agency. First I was just with them as a client picking up extra gigs for commercials or movies. This didn't pay well and I knew I had to find a full time job. I was getting further and further into debt yet I didn't give up. I cried a lot, almost everyday. The talent agency took me on full time in the office as an agent and I loved working with Art, but the owner hated me and I never quite understood why. Art was my friend, a gay older man who was just the coolest guy! He always gave great advice; he is why I stuck it out there. The agency was a real trip. Hundreds and hundreds of people who want to make it big in the biz and would do anything to do so. I was one of them, yet I also knew my chances were slim; so much competition, I felt so small. The calls would come in and we would look on the wall and in files and fill the casting calls. I think I went on only two calls, and one I got. The owner thought I was a nothing and when Art wanted to cast me for this part he really had to talk Steve into it. Finally he gave in and said I would do well casting for this part since it was a bar whore casting and that is one thing I would be good at. I did get the part; it was in a national commercial for the armed forces. I really loved doing that, it was much fun and also brought Della and Cindy into my life. I met a lot of people at the job, mostly all superficial. I didn't care. I just wanted some friends; I was so alone. I met Lynette at the agency. She worked down the hall and she and I became friends fast. We hung out a lot.

One gig I did was a commercial for tennis; I was an extra for this gig and I had to sit in the bleachers for hours. I ended up meeting this guy and, after hours of talking, I find out a friend of his was this guy I went to high school with. This guy used to come over to my house and help me roll joints when I was selling pot. I was thrilled and we set it up so I could see him again. That encounter was perfect. I needed a familiar face to keep going. Don, his roommates and I got along great. All of us became good friends and partied together. I eventually introduced Lynette to Don and they started going out. Things started to fall apart with Lynette and I after she hooked up with Don. I continued to be depressed daily!

The pay wasn't good at the agency; I was always looking for something to bring in some money. I got into the wedding business shooting second camera for weddings and that was a total joke, not to mention the money was shit. I would always run second camera and the guys were always bossy and plain stupid! I knew I was more than qualified after working in cable for six years producing commercials, yet I couldn't get a job anywhere doing that. Most people didn't even believe that my demo reel was mine. I was also told I did too much and that I needed to pick one thing I was good at and stick with that. Wall after wall, it was endless!

Desperate one night I called an escort service, the one where I get paid to go on a date. On the phone with these people they asked my age and said not to lie; I didn't, I was 29 and the woman said I was too old! Too old? Too old to fuck? I was so livid. She said the guys want the girls young and

I was too old and that was that! I hung up crying, thinking I can't even get a job like that. I'm 29, twenty-nine! This put me on a quest. I was terribly insecure and depressed; I was only twenty-nine and not even wanted by men! I was so mentally fucked up. I went and applied for a job as a topless waitress, I knew I had the tits!

I go in for this so called interview and the guy comes in, tells me to spin, then tells me to come back after I lose 10 pounds! Okay, now I am really losing it! I actually tried to lose weight, and then decided fuck it. I didn't think I could pull off doing lap dances, anyway. So, I was browsing through the paper and I found an ad for someone to clean and work on this yacht. I called the number and set up an interview. I get over to the house and an old man on a breathing machine opens the door. Before I am two feet in, he offers me a beer! A beer at an interview? I have to admit I have been a bit wild in my day, but I was always very professional and kept my work life and my personal life separate. Drinking at an interview just disturbed me. We were sitting at this table and out of the back window there is this young man cleaning the pool. The old man starts in on what the job really details. I will get to the point, he wanted me to masturbate in front of him and he would pay me. I said no way, and then he asks if I will get it on with the pool boy while he watches. Again, I declined. I was feeling like I needed to get the hell out of there and needed to do it very gently. He knew that I worked at a talent agency and pulled out these photos of really young girls, say, around eleven to fourteen years old. He asks if I will bring him young girls, that he really prefers the young ones. He says he gets his hands on these young girls all of the time and he will pay me to send them to him. I was totally blown away, yet I kept it together. I told him what he wanted to hear just so I could get out! Depressed isn't even the word now, I was devastated. I am not a stupid girl, yet I am always amazed at what people do! I play naïve just to get the fuck out without any problems, it seems to work!

I ended up getting involved with a woman that was a total scam artist. I went and worked on a pilot all night long for this Spanish show, what a joke that was. I never did get my pay for this gig, the woman split town. I was at her office when a man drove up in a really expensive car with a young thing on his side. The girl went in. I was outside and he called me over to the car. You see, I wasn't afraid of anything. I wanted so bad to make it big, yet I knew I would only go so far. This guy went on and on about how important he was; that he worked on big films, with the likes of

Tom Cruise. He just couldn't say enough about how great he was. He told me to call him to talk about how I could break into the business. Shit, I would do grip, I would do whatever on set; just get me in and the rest will speak for itself. So I called the guy and set up an appointment. His office was in Miami, I went all dressed up and ready! The guy was a joke as they all were. This one wanted to put me up in an apartment and pay my way. He didn't really want sex, just wanted blowjobs. He said he did this for many girls to give them a start. He didn't get the fact that I actually wanted to work, not be his whore. He was creepy; he had long nails with polish. I remember him coming around the desk and putting his hands on my shoulders and talking dirty to me. I thought, "He has a cane, if I have to run I can get away." He did make many promises; there was a part of me that thought about it for a moment. Give a piece of me away to get the job. He was so full of shit though. He felt women didn't have a place in the business except for being sluts. He called and harassed me for a long time, kept making all of these promises and I kept running the other way. Eventually he, too, gave up.

I ended up leaving the talent agency for a better paying job at an on-hold company. Art told me to be careful and that money wasn't everything. He thought the owner was tough and he didn't think I had the backbone for it. He was right. It didn't take me long to figure that out, but the guy was paying $500 a week cash to read on-hold messages. I thought how easy, I've been in radio, I did have a great voice and I knew I could do this job. I was never good enough for this gig. When the voice work went to New York, people bitched about my Midwest accent; in the South they bitched about it too. I just couldn't win, unless of course it was being played in the Midwest. The owner was a fucking asshole. To this day I can remember how mean and cruel he was to me. He just hated women; that was obvious. Boca and I worked together; he was a local "popular" guy in radio and humor. He liked me; too much maybe. He was also a bit manipulative to getting his way. I cried everyday I came home from this job. It just didn't seem to matter how hard I worked or tried to meet their standards. The main guy cut my pay. To this day, I can't remember why? He was always just so mean to me, the things he said: "dumb," "blonde," and "worthless." I hated this job, yet did what I had to, to survive. Finally I lost it with my boss' cruel words and just blew up. I went off on the bastard and walked out, quit!

During this gig, Boca wanted to hook me up with a friend of his. I wasn't so sure about it since he had told me some stories that were a bit disturbing about the guy. The guy was a millionaire and I thought what the hell. I decided to drive to this date just in case I needed a way out, and it turns out I did. We met at a restaurant and the first thing this fuck said to me was, "I am picturing you in a strap on dildo," like that turned me on ☺. I decided to stomach my way through the meal when he invited me back to his house. Now mind you, his home was featured on Forbes, so I knew I had to see this house. I followed him back to his house. At this point I will do my best to remember what took place. I wasn't drunk at all; I was sober. His home was incredible, huge! He gave me a tour. In the backyard he tried to get a hold of my tits and I turned him away. He then proceeded to show me the rest of the house. I swear every room he showed me had something to do with sex; sex, room after room. I was sitting on the couch about to leave, and he excused himself for a moment. He came back into the room naked with a gold cock ring on. He sat next to me and I was just frozen. He then decided to jack off as I was sitting there. He finished, left the room and I got up and got the hell out of there; never to look back. I cried all the way home. I actually stopped at a bar to drink my sorrows away.

I spent a lot of time drinking my sorrows away. So much rejection; the guys just didn't like me in Florida. I was too fat, my tits were too big; whatever excuse they could come up with. I met quite a few men that I liked, but they just didn't have any feelings for me. So things were really sucking by now, I quit my job and was back begging the agency to help me out. I did one gig on the street with a sandwich board on to promote a business. The cops came and shut that down, so I only got half my pay. I was doing odd jobs when I met Para, a young actress trying to make it big as well. I met her on the set for Donny Brasco, she and I were extras. This was fun. I loved the film work, even if I was an extra. It was the first time I ever saw Al Pacino in person, along with Johnny Depp and the Mike guy who is pretty famous as well. I remember well making eye contact with Pacino. I used to think if someone would just look at me they would see something special and I would become famous. They would take the time to see how talented I actually was. Yeah, right? Anyway, I was going up the escalator and Al Pacino was coming down. I was facing the other direction and this guy yells, "It's Al, hey Al? It's Al Pacino!" He turned back and looked right into my eyes and winked at me, I about fell off the escalator!

The movie was fun. It was very competitive among the extras, yet fun! So, Para and I became friends and she introduced me to this marketing company, where you do sampling programs for new products. She needed some samplers to go to Georgia to do a promotion. This sounded like fun, so Della, Para and a few others got into Della's car and went to Georgia. The promotion was fun, but I didn't want to be a sampler; I wanted to be the boss. I called the company to apply for Para's position and they said they could really use me, but not in Florida. I had to go back to Michigan and they would get me started. That was it for me; I had to get the hell out of Florida and now was the time. I decided to make the move after Christmas. My parents and Eddie were coming down to visit. Eddie was going to help me move back.

Just one story I think I should tell before I head out of Florida. When Eddie came to visit, I introduced him to Lynette's sister Julie. They hit it off and got together. One night a bunch of us were to go out and party. Right in the middle of the party, Eddie wanted to leave to be alone with Julie. Lynette wanted to leave to meet up with Dave. I was left alone at the rave. I ended up getting extremely depressed and decided once again that I wanted to die. I left the bar, totally fucked up and walked all the way to the beach. I called and left a message for Eddie that I was going to walk and walk, right into the ocean until I drowned. I did walk all the way to the water, and then I collapsed on the beach and passed out. I woke up at some point to a guy sitting next to me. It was weird; he said that he didn't want to leave my side, that he was there to watch over me. We sat there a while and then I heard Eddie's voice screaming for me. I got up, ran to Eddie and he took me home.

There was this one guy that I met while working at the agency and he gave me something of value that I still have today. He had it laminated for me and this was so huge. Here I will share what the poster says and you will understand why it had such an impact:

Desiderata

Go placidly amid the noise and the haste, and remember what peace their may be in silence-As far as possible without surrender, be on good terms with all persons-Speak your truth quietly and clearly; and listen to others, even the dull and the ignorant; they too have their story-Avoid loud and aggressive persons, they are vexations to the spirit-if you compare yourself with others, you may become vain and bitter, for always there will be greater and lesser persons than yourself. Enjoy your achievements as well as your plans-Keep interested in your own career, however humble; it is a real possession in the changing fortunes of time-Exercise caution in your business affairs, for the world is full of trickery-But do not let this blind you to what truth there is; many persons strive for high ideals; and everywhere Life is full of heroism-Be yourself-Especially do not feign affection-Neither be cynical about Love, for in the face of all aridity and disenchantment, it is still as perennial as the grass-Take kindly to the counsel of years, gratefully surrendering the things of youth-Nurture strength of spirit to shield you in sudden misfortune. But do not stress yourself with imagining-Many fears are born of fatigue and loneliness-Beyond a wholesome discipline, be gentle with yourself-You are a Child of the Universe, no less than the trees and stars; you have a right to be here-And whether or not it is clear to you no doubt the Universe is unfolding as it should-Therefore, be at peace with your God, whatever you conceive Him to be and whatever your labors and aspirations in the noisy confusion of Life keep peace with your soul-With all its sham, drudgery and broken dreams, it is still a beautiful world-Be careful-Strive to be happy-Anonymous

My days in Florida were long and hard. I was depressed constantly. I never did meet any people that were true friends. They were all so shallow and backstabbing. I just couldn't take it anymore and I knew I had to give it up! So I did; Eddie and I packed up everything and I moved back to Grand Rapids, not even one year later.

Chapter Nine

When I got back to Grand Rapids I got into a small apartment. This marketing company came through and gave me my first promotion for a soft drink. I did this for two weeks. It was busy, crazy and fun. The money was pretty good, so I decided to do more work with this marketing company. A lady that I worked with at cable wanted to leave her boyfriend and move in with me. I was in a one bedroom at this time, but I knew I would be traveling so I agreed to her moving in. After the soft drink promotion, I went to North Carolina to do a drink for old people. This is where I met Natasha; she was a sampler for me. This is also where I met Don. Don owned a traveling candy store. He and I really liked each other. He was really flirting with me and thought I would be great at selling his product. Natasha and I hit it off so well that I stayed at her house out in the country. She was married to a complete asshole, but I liked her. I felt sorry for her really. Her husband was very mean and bossy to her, very controlling, yet she stuck with it. We became good friends, although her husband just hated me. Don wanted me to take a ride to Virginia Beach to check out his company. He had a booth set up and wanted to see how I would do running it. I went up for the weekend and that's how I got involved with his company. It's also how Don and I got involved sexually I gave the marketing company a break and decided that after North Carolina I wanted to move to Virginia and work for Don. He offered good pay as well. My roommate and I moved into a two bedroom. I didn't want to totally move everything to Virginia just in case it didn't work out. I took Schekki with me. I packed up just the Toyota this time and Mom decided to go along with me for the first couple of weeks; good 'ol Mom! Don was to set me up in an apartment. When we finally got there, the apartment that he found was actually the basement of this house. The owners were from the country of India. The little space wasn't at all set up like an apartment.

They said it was furnished; yet there was just a piece of wood on the floor that I was to sleep on. You couldn't even get into the kitchen; I had to slide in sideways to do the dishes. There was no stove, just a heating thing, and stairs that went up to the owner's house with a door that didn't lock. The room was seven hundred dollars a month, which was fucked up! I hated this place. We were there one day and Schekki managed to get stuck up in the rafters. He wouldn't come down; I was panicked! He never liked it there. Mom and I made due and I started working for Don. Mom went on a few shows with me and that was nice. One show in Virginia I met this guy Cary, a really nice guy that said I could come live with him. Mom felt good about this guy, since my current living conditions were a nightmare. Mom and I made the best of the shows. I would drive to Don's warehouse and pick up crates and crates of candy that he loaded into a trailer I pulled behind my truck. In truth it was a lot of hard work. It was really nice having my mom there to help me out and when I dropped her off at the airport she hugged me, teary eyed, and said get the hell out of that apartment! She was right and I knew it. The young man that lived in the house had been sneaking down in my room when we were gone and going through my stuff. He had a major crush on me; he thought American women were interesting. He was married, but told me that it was okay since he is allowed to have more than one wife! God! I had to get the fuck out of there and I did. As soon as I could, I moved in with Cary. The move took me further from the pickup office and Don wasn't too thrilled since he wanted to see me on demand. I was fucking him right in the warehouse, his wife never knew. So I kept doing the shows, going all over the place, picking up cases and cases of product and driving all over, setting up a booth and selling candy all by myself. Driving the 4-Runner with a trailer behind me, what a nightmare that was! I finally had enough. The last show

I did Don asked me to take along this girl that was in training. It rained liked crazy the first day of the show so I decided to not go. No one was even there. I guess that was not a good idea because they threw me out of the show. That night the girl I was training had met this guy and decided while I was sleeping to steal my truck and go out to meet this guy. I woke up, my truck was gone, she was gone and I panicked. I didn't know what to do, she was a bit crazy and I thought for sure she was gone for good. I paced, made phone calls and waited it out, finally she showed up and I just lost it! I was done! Done with this bullshit! Cary was a great roommate, we became good friends, yet I just couldn't do the candy thing anymore and the pay all of a sudden just wasn't good enough for the kind of work that I was doing! I decided to pack it up and head back home. Don was pissed that I left and tried to hold my last paycheck. I threatened him by saying that I would tell his wife; that didn't seem to work, he did a stop payment on the check and I went to my Dad for advice. Dad did up the necessary paperwork to sue him for the money, he sent it in and we had our court date set. Mom, Dad and I had breakfast the morning that Dad and I were to head off to Virginia to get my last paycheck. Dad had sued him for the last check plus all the travel fees, so it was worth it to make the journey for my money. We were having breakfast and Dad tossed a piece of paper across the table. I opened it up and it was a check! The check was more than what we were suing Don for! Dad had the check in hand for a few days, but wanted to surprise me! Surprise me he did! Whew, no long ass road trip with Dad!

I was back in Grand Rapids living with a roommate and that situation was not working out. I thought it would be fine since I was traveling; yet she was a major pothead, smoking day and night. She was very lazy. I got a gig with my old marketing company to go back to North Carolina to do a chocolate drink promotion. I went back and stayed with Natasha as she helped me with the promotion. One day after a set-up, we came back to her house and we had to back in the big trailer (it looked like a big bottle). I forgot to secure the tires before I unhooked the trailer and I climbed in the back. All of a sudden I felt the trailer lift and move. I opened the door and realized I was moving down hill, I jumped out and ran around the front and grabbed the trailer. It started going pretty fast and it drug me down the hill, over stones and cement. Natasha came running out and tried to stop it from the side. Just before it landed in the river it stopped dead by a tree, inches from the water. My heart was pounding so fast and I was really torn up. I still have shoulder problems to this day from that.

Anyway, the trailer stopped, thank God! She and I really enjoyed doing this gig, we were pretty well known in town as the two hot babes driving the trailer. We were even invited on a very popular radio show for an interview. That was way cool. This promotion lasted maybe a month and then I went back home to wait for my new assignment. When I got home, I remember trying to keep in touch with Natasha, but something weird happened. She wouldn't talk to me. I finally got her to say what was going on. She found out that her husband had crabs and he blamed it on me, not that we had sex, but that I got it on the sheets and he got it that way. She actually believed him! He didn't want me around her anymore; I was a bad influence. God forbid that she feels good about herself. I was always pumping her up, she needed to feel good and beautiful and I did that! Jim always knocked her down and kept her under his thumb, but this blew me away that she believed him. I'm sure he got it from another women, but I know for sure it wasn't me. That was the end of my relationship with Natasha; I have never spoken with her since. Pretty sad really, I liked Natasha.

10-23-97

I spent the entire summer in Upstate New York, driving a twenty-four foot truck. Broke down, men jacking off, truck robbed, it was a wild two months. Met a lot of wonderful people. Andy in Connecticut, Brian in Albany, my Pepsi guy in Syracuse, a couple experiences for sure!! All exciting! My limo ride back to Albany, hotel to hotel, crazy work. Came home and three weeks later took off for Massachusetts, mainly Boston, doing another promotion. Stayed 1 month, Eliza was great; she is a stress case, but a sweetie and young! New England is beautiful in the fall. Went to Maine and partied it up good! Boston is a busy city, so, so much to do! I was pretty good, didn't meet any men, just some female bonding. Anyway now I'm back deciding what now, I'm tired of the marketing company and I'm gonna try for getting my own biz started and well, still alone. I really love traveling; I just need to make some money! I'm very happy though! Free spirit and loving life and living it! No one gets too close. I guess if it ever happens for me, I will know, as for now, I need to grow. Grampa is doing ok, parents are good, I just miss family. Being on the road can wear on me, you know. I'll be in touch- you know me, not to dedicated to anything!

That diary entry is a quick way to sum up an entire summer. I took this big job with the marketing company in Upstate New York doing a sampling program for another soft drink. I have to say that after that promotion, I will never drink another one of those. It was a really wild time going from hotel to hotel. I did a big pick up at a warehouse and had a really bad feeling about how the truck was running. I begged this guy that loaded my truck to come with me. I had some people out at this lake doing sampling and I had to leave them to go pick up more products. My gut instincts were right; we were on the busiest highway possible when the truck broke down. He was a pretty cool guy and we made some phone calls to get help. In the waiting time we smoked a joint. It was hotter than hell and we waited a really long time. The cops showed up and that was interesting considering I wasn't licensed to pull that much weight. He ended up letting it go and left us to wait for the tow truck. I have never in my life seen such a big tow truck. In the process of hooking up the truck all of the pallets of soda came crashing down. That was one big mess. I knew I wasn't even going to try to sample this product, so I found a frat house and donated every single can to them as long as they helped me unload it all. There was a good chance that if this marketing company ever knew about this I would have been fired on the spot, but I didn't give a shit. I called them to help me out and they did nothing, I almost quit that job right then and there. I'm not a quitter though, so I kept going. I did meet a lot of men on this trip; one in particular was Ryan. I met Ryan at a show. He sold pottery that he did himself. I had seen him at a few shows already when I was doing the candy thing and we had become friends/lovers. I remember Don sending me off to New York City alone and I got lost in a really bad part of town. I couldn't find a hotel and it was getting really late. I was in tears driving all over when I finally found one that had an open room. I didn't even get 2 hours of sleep before I had to be up and at the show. Once I got there and got set up I was asking around to see if anyone knew of a room I could get since I had to do this show for 2 days. This old goat tells me the town is sold out but I can share his room and sleep on the couch! I was thinking he wasn't gonna mess with me, but sure enough he tried. I roll over and there he is next to me trying to get a feel. I squirmed away and told him he was just to old and I was not interested. Ryan was at this show. We started bonding right away. I knew of all the shows that he was doing and we always managed to hook up and see each other. He was my savior that night. When I was doing the whole upstate tour, he and I managed to put some shows together so we could see each other. I wasn't dedicated to Ryan; he was married. I had my share of men throughout this entire trip.

One night, being at the hotel, I decided to go for a drink. There was a wedding at the hotel and one of the groomsmen started hitting on me. I ended up taking him back to my room; he and I stayed in touch during my summer travels, but once I got home, I ended that. He was such a nice guy. He sent me a dozen roses when I got home. I liked him, but he was too into a relationship and I knew it would never work. We had our fun while it lasted. It was all fun to me, I didn't want to owe anyone anything. I had a meeting with this company and the general manager took me out for a beer. One thing led to another and I ended up giving him a blowjob; he too was married. I drove that big ass truck back to my hotel all fucked up. It surprises me even today that I made it back!

I did have some down time and this one time I wanted to go to the Syracuse racetracks. This guy kept following me around and finally we started to talk. He had ditched his wife to make a pass at me. It turned out we were staying in the same hotel. That night, after I went to bed, he was good and drunk and decided to run down the hallway screaming my name to find out what room I was in! I stayed hidden until they left!

New York was really amazing to me in many ways. Here I am out on my own, running a twenty-four foot truck, packing pallets of product. I dropped a ton of weight during this summer loading cases and cases of this soft drink. It was an exhausting job, but it always gave me this incredible feeling that I could do and handle anything. I had plenty of time to think when I wasn't filling my time with men and booze. One set up I will never forget was in this dirty little city. It could have been Syracuse, I can't remember, but I do remember that it was an awful place to set up a truck with hundreds of cases of soda. There was a lot of poverty here. The bums would come up for a sample and I would give them the whole case if they could carry it. This one guy I really felt sorry for. He was huge, his legs were all swollen and purple, his feet were mangled and nasty. His clothes were so dirty. I just wanted to give him whatever he could handle. He took 3 cases and I didn't think he would get to far. When he turned to go, his pants were all piss stained and he had shit running down his leg. I walked away at one point only to return to a truck gone wild. One of the samplers let the bums up in the truck to take whatever they wanted. The truck was full of people grabbing and running; things got pretty out of hand. This of course is a major NO-NO! One sample per person! I knew we would never meet our numbers with one sample per person, so I encouraged the samplers to do what they had to so we could get done early and get paid the same! They loved me!

After New York I was sent to Boston for a mouthwash promotion. Eliza was my partner and we worked very well together. When we were loading the truck, I was on the edge and the guys were throwing me boxes. I missed my step and fell between the loading dock and the truck. My arm came up and supported my head otherwise I'm sure I would have cracked my head open. I was really disoriented for a while. This was about a month long promotion. Not much excitement on this trip, though later I heard that one of the guys that worked for us had overdosed on crack cocaine and died. I knew that this would be my last promotion. It was time to move on.

Chapter Ten

When I got home I knew I was done with all that and I really wanted to get focused on my own business. My roomate and I were not getting along; we didn't live well together. She always had her grandkid over and you know me with kids. It was just one thing after another. I seemed to be taking care of everything. Shit, I got home and knew right away something was wrong with Schekki. I took him in and he was blocked and was going to die if I didn't cough up $600 for the surgery. Now how can a person not notice that the cat hadn't peed in weeks? This really pissed me off; she was to be watching over him when I was gone. I did so many jobs that I thought it best I didn't tote Schekki all around with me; she was to care for him. She was just so incompetent. It really bothered me.

I wasn't going to be traveling anymore for the marketing company and I knew my roomate and I just couldn't live together. I had tried to make the best of it! I didn't want any conflict, but I'm the type of person who will keep things bottled up until I explode. Eventually I exploded, but not before I met Darin and went to Europe. I went to Texas, first, with my mom. My Grandpa was dying and I had to be with him. This was a really hard time for me. I so loved my Gramps. He was the greatest and watching him lie on that bed just tore me up. I hated to leave, when I got home I turned around and went to Europe with Darin. I met Darin when I was working part time as a bartender. He has an attention problem; I think they call it ADD. I did like him, but he got on my nerves really fast. I could only take so much of him. He wanted to take me to Europe and, well, how could I resist?

I had to get a job doing something while I considered opening my production company, so I started bartending. I was terrible at it. I heard of this place that was hiring. It was a news and traffic position for many radio stations. I got the job with no problem at all. I took Mr. ADD up on his offer to go to Europe and he said he would handle and pay for everything. I was so excited about going I didn't even consider who I was going to be stuck with. Actually I didn't care; I just wanted to go to Europe on someone else's tab. I even made it clear to him that going didn't mean we were in some kind of relationship; I had sex with him a few times and knew he would expect that. I figured I could handle that. He was the type of guy that always had to be touching me, next to me constantly. I had no space of my own. He was very possessive with me and I just couldn't stand it! I was someone that always wanted attention, yet not like this and not by him. I wanted attention and was challenged by guys that didn't give me attention. The silly things the mind does, crazy!

Darin and I headed off to Europe for the longest plane ride of my life. I loved to fly, but alone. Having this man that wouldn't shut the fuck up made a twelve-hour flight seem like a lifetime. I would have loved Europe more if I traveled alone or with someone else. I couldn't do anything by myself. I found myself wanting to sleep or get drunk just to deal with it! We went over to Paris for a few days. I loved Paris; not so much the people though. We celebrated the New Year in front of the Eiffel tower then spent until dawn trying to get a cab to take us back. Not fun! I think that most of the time I was thinking about my Grandpa and I just couldn't have a good time. One night back in London, I went to bed and this is what I remember, I went into a dream. In the dream I was on the elevator and it kept going up higher. The doors would open and shut. I got to the highest floor and the doors opened; my grandpa was standing on the other side, he had his arms open and I reached out for him. I wanted to take a step forward but knew I couldn't cross. He just smiled and said I couldn't go, then he said goodbye. I woke up on the other side of the room. This is what Darin told me: he said I was in the corner of the room with my arms open wide, talking. He kept saying my name until I finally woke up. I was dumbfounded, standing there, trying to piece it together. In that instant I knew my grandpa passed. I called back to my mom in Michigan who confirmed that he did die and by the way it timed out, his passing was when I went into my dream state. I cried so hard. I went into the bathroom and locked the door; I just wanted to be left alone. Darin had made arrangements to go see the *Phantom of the Opera* and I really didn't have it in me to go. After crying all day I finally got my shit together and went. It was a great show; I'm glad I went.

Things started to really change for me after my favorite Gramps died. I started to have a huge interest in death and what this life really is. I sang at his funeral and barely made it through *Amazing Grace* before I fell apart. I haven't really experienced much death in my life, so I never really thought about it. I decided it was time to make death a part of my waking life. I don't believe in heaven or hell; I dropped that whole thing a while back but the spiritual programming was pretty strong and I still wasn't sure what or who I was. At this point I still believed in God; not sure what, just a god that controlled everything. Honestly, I was so confused. I didn't know anything but decided I would like to start inquiring and stop believing everything I heard or was told.

Once I got home from Europe I dumped Darin cold! He kept calling and coming around but I just ignored him until finally he got the hint.

After Andy and I had been divorced I decided it was time for me. I knew I wanted to do my traveling; I did the Club Med thing twice, the second one was Martinique. That was one big orgy. It was so crazy I had guys all over me day and night and I got really tired of that quick. I decided after that trip (that I was drunk for the entire time) that it was the last of my Club Med traveling. I also dreamed of owning my own Corvette. I actually bought a 1977 Corvette that I loved and when I moved to Florida I had it brought down to me. Things got pretty bad in Florida with money so I ended up selling it (kind of) to this guy I dated for a minute. He really just took over the payments. Once I got home to Michigan, he was doing ok on the payments for a while but then he started to default. I was starting to get my financial world back together, so this guy I met at a gas station and I flew to Florida and drove the Corvette back. I ended up giving it to my dad to make the payments since I still couldn't afford them.

I think about that now, and what it was like for this guy to go out to his car and find it gone. The repo place had told me the car was trashed and to just let it go. I had to pay them $500 to repossess it and they said it wasn't even worth that anymore. I didn't believe them and I'm glad I didn't because that car was well cared for, better off then when I turned it over. Kerry is this guy I met when I stopped for cigs or gas. He worked in the station and got up the nerve to ask me out. He was a good ten years younger than me, but I liked him. He looked like Val Kilmer with long hair, and he had a voice like Creed. I agreed and we just ended up hanging out all the time. He was really a creative guy. He wrote poetry and music. One of those guys that are so talented but never gets noticed. I think that really was hard on him. He was never happy and spent most of his time depressed and stoned, not to mention he had a temper. He was living in some shack with his cousin and since we were together all the time I invited him to move in. Kerry also had this bible reading side. I was never into the bible, but he started getting me to believe in it. I actually started going to church. I felt I needed something to keep me positive; I hadn't thrown "the roommate" out yet and she was so very negative I couldn't take it anymore.

She and I got into a huge fight and I threw her ass out. Now I was living alone with Kerry and that didn't last too long. Kerry helped me get my business started and he did some shooting and editing; he was actually good at it, but he hated it. He didn't do well with people; he was better closed up in a room alone. Me, I'm social; so we were butting heads quite often. I ended up buying him a car and he just made the payments, this ended up working just fine. He never left me to pick up the tab.

I was working as a news reporter, which I really didn't care for. I was also getting my production company up and running. Things started taking off for the company and I knew at some point I would want to dedicate my full time to the business. Doing news has got to be the most depressing gig on this planet. I have no interest in politics, sports, or any of it really and there I was doing it. What I was good at was being on the air. It was a good job that paid the bills and had its share of sexual harassment as well.

This guy was so ridiculous. I would go on the air and right behind me he would start changing his clothes. One time he came up behind me and ran his hands down my shirt. Another time he cornered me in the elevator. This guy was married with like seven kids. At one point I mentioned this to a co-worker and she took it upon herself to report him. I was called into the office with the big wigs and I did tell them what was going on. This guy ended up getting fired and taking another job in television in the same town. I heard he was doing the same thing at his new job, but made a horrible mistake by typing this very sexual email to this girl and accidentally sending it out to everyone at the station. He was fired again! His wife was in total denial. She use to call me and make personal threats, saying it was my fault he was fired. In her and his minds, I'm sure it was my fault.

Things started to fall apart with Kerry and I. This is a piece from how I was feeling in that moment:

Things aren't so great in the relationship and I don't really know how to explain! Our lives are going separate. He has no interest in my friends so we go our own ways. Really, there is so much more, and it makes me sad, but if I'm not being fulfilled, then maybe it's time. I have spent so much time alone, and now I have someone in my life and I feel even lonelier. I think and think until my head aches and all I feel is this emptiness. My life is so strange; all the feelings mixed up, and then wham! It's over! He doesn't want to spend time with me. He wants to work part-time and play full time, but not with me. I have got to let this anger go. He has his life and I have mine. I promise to never let another control me this way and look, it's happening. It's a challenge every day and I'm tired. I have the good Lord with me and that is all I need, to know he is watching over me, to feel his strength in me, my mom says I can't be alone, but what's the catch? I am alone. I do have me and I love myself. There are things I need to work on; I will always be working on ways to improve myself. I need to do it. I want to be loved deeply; this is life and life in the 90s. I'm not afraid. I'm just waiting for the Lord to come and take me home. Home to real love and real happiness. This life is only temporary? Miss you Gramps!

I guess, when reading that, that Kerry's religious stuff was working. When I read the Jesus stuff now it makes me nauseous. Kerry and I decided it was time for him to move out. We were still friends, we never fought about it, we both just knew. He ended up moving back to Georgia. He and I kept in touch but mainly because he owed me money, which he did pay. After the payments were done I never heard from him again. I suppose if he ever made it big, I would know. Too bad really, he was a great talent.

I was now living totally alone… oh yeah, I do have my Schekki; can't forget him. The business was doing pretty good. I used Kim, a friend in radio, and a few other guys to help me shoot once in awhile. My neighbors were two guys that were partners. Ron a forty-something white guy and Charles a fifty-something black guy. Ron and I were better friends; he did some shooting for me once in awhile. Charles eventually liked me; at first he was just leery of people and their judgments. I never cared about how they wanted to live. Ron and I became good friends. He hung out with me a lot and I would guess he and I were both pretty fucked up and that's why we got along. Talk about drama! First, he has to deal with being gay in this very anti-gay world and second with a black man. He loved black men; they were his only interest. He and Charles were not even close to being loyal to one another. Ron was always out with other guys, but his choice was black. I had the pleasure of learning more about this world and it fascinated me. I would go out with Ron to his gay bars and if he couldn't go I would go alone. I loved the gay scene. No one gave a shit about me and no one hit on me. Ron and I had some fun. He struggled a lot with what the bible had to say about being gay and I use to say it was bullshit. I can't imagine, even if there were a god, he would care what your sexual preferences were. And to burn in hell for it? Give me a break.

I believe his mom was some kind of pastor. It was really hard for him and we would talk for hours about it, but it didn't seem to matter. He remained in the closet for a long time. He was a painter by trade and no one ever knew he was gay. He liked it that way; but what a way to live, lying and hiding all the time. Then again if he came out of the closet he would have had other things to deal with. I just tried to be a good friend.

I was starting to pick up a lot of weddings and I was still partying pretty hard. I remember doing this one wedding and getting so fucked up, I can't remember what happened. I hooked up with some guy and I remember coming to in the stairwell at the hotel alone. I blacked out. This is when my drinking started to take me into the black. Where my memory fails me. To wake up and have no idea where you are and who you were with. This became quite common, even though I thought I was getting my life together. I was reading more spiritual books and trying to get in touch with my true self. My desire for social work was big; I needed to be invited to all of the parties, I needed to be accepted. While working at the news station I became friends with Dick and Sandy. Sandy did traffic with me and Dick was the artist boyfriend. There was a good twenty years between them, but they seemed to work.

I moved into a townhouse to have more space for the business. I am using my diary as reference to remind me of what I was doing and how. My life at this point is a bit interesting. I'm not interested in boring you with all of the jabber on how many men I brought home; either from weddings, the bar or wherever. I would then wake up the next day and try to be all connected spiritually and make every excuse possible for my behavior. I was never at ease in my head. Every moment was a struggle between doing what's right and living on purpose. One moment I thought I had it figured out, the next I was depressed and crying. If things didn't go my way I would just get trashed. I was constantly filling voids, one after another to validate myself. I filtered through men like it was nothing. It was nothing; I just tried to make it something. What's surprising is that I kept the business going and that it was doing well. I met these two guys that roomed together when I took the townhouse. They were totally into coke and it was prime! We did coke all day and night, and then the next day. That night I had a wedding. I was trying to come down some hours before, but I was just to wired. It was a two-camera gig; I took the balcony so I wouldn't be around people. My nose was draining like crazy and I felt like shit so I would sneak to the bathroom, blow my nose and snort up some more coke (I had plenty of time since it was a Catholic wedding). I knew I couldn't finish this gig so I had my assistant do the reception. I remember playing like I had allergies and going home. I still could not sleep. I hated feeling like this. The thing is, I was so out of my coked up head that the camera was not recording right and the entire ceremony was messed up digitally. I did my best in editing, but in the end I had to refund the money to the client. They weren't happy and neither was I! I was so upset with myself for being so sloppy and not caring about my business! I swore to clean up my act and to never ever do this again; I didn't. Yes, I did coke again, but never did I carry any of this into my professional world again. I stopped drinking at the weddings. It was business and I held to it!

Chapter Eleven

I booked a big gig with my company, a $10,000 gig; the first biggie and it really was a nightmare. I never turned down work. "Can't" never did anything is what my dad always said. I would do it one way or another. This gig was for a school. My contact was Shari, I liked her yet she forgot everything she said from one moment to the next; there was no direction in the scripting of the project. I would work for hours on shooting and editing pieces, and then she would come by and change the whole idea; wanting me to start over again. Things got pretty bad so I called in a mediator. We finally got to a point where I turned the job over and it was done. They paid me an agreed upon amount, this took a really long time to finish. I was so depressed through the transition. I wanted so badly to do a great job with this gig and things were just out of control. I had to let it go and move on to other projects.

The next big project was a commercial for a popcorn shop. They wanted something really great; $3,200 for a 30 second commercial, I was so excited to do something creative. I wrote a jingle with a friend and hired dancers, it was to be a big production! The night before the big commercial shoot I went to a black tie party at Dick and Sandy's. Joe, the guy that helped write the jingle (and was acting in the spot) was there as well. Dick and Sandy had many gay friends; Joe was one of them who I just loved! We had a great time and decided to keep the party going by doing some bar hopping. I was pretty drunk and stoned by the time Joe and I headed home. I remember trying so hard to keep the truck on the road. My vision was really distorted and I was hitting the curbs and swerving really bad. I was one block from my apartment and I got pulled over. Here I am in my long evening gown, hair up, looking good but totally smashed. In high heels they ask me to do the big walk the line thing, which I failed. Again, it was the good cop, bad cop scenario. Again, the bad cop won. I was cuffed and hauled off to jail. I put up one hell of a verbal argument; telling the cops to fuck off, that I had done so much for them and this is the shit I get. When that didn't work, I tried the sex approach. Nothing worked, it only made things worse I'm sure. I tried everything to keep me out of a jail cell. I tried to make a bunch of phone calls: I called Eddie to bail me out; I called Kim to tell her to cancel the shoot and then faked a few more. Eventually they put me in a cell with a bunch of girls. One girl pretty much demanded my $200 suit overcoat from the dress, and to avoid a fight, I gave it to her. They finally let me go when Eddie got there; I was still drunk. This time I didn't blame anyone but myself. Who else was there to blame? I once again lost my license; I hired an attorney this time and ended up paying a ton of money. It's all about money anyway. They put me on eighty hours of community service and when I did one day of painting rich people's curbs, I flat out refused to go back! I told the judge I had more to offer than that and he let me do free video work for this company. When it came time to actually do the work, they never wanted to use me so they just told the court I did it and it was done! This is a funny story to me. This company that I was to do some free work for was working on a non-profit production and if they let me do free work they wouldn't have made any money. They would rather lie to the court and tell them that I did the community service than have me involved. Non-profit is such a scam. I learned much about this during my enquiry. Non-profit is nothing more than a business, and a big business at that!

I ended up booking a flight to Vegas for a conference on video production; I thought I should check out what everyone else was doing. I ended up partying with different men every night and blowing off half of the convention. It was boring and my work was totally as good. The first night

I picked up this black man about half my age and took him back to my hotel room. We just fooled around, and once I got a look at what was hiding in his pants I didn't want anything to do with it(and Ken said I would never find a man with a bigger cock!). He was a really nice guy and stayed with me all night, but the rest of the trip I avoided him. I met these guys from New York and we all went to see George Carlin. I loved George Carlin, he was so right on; but I can't begin to tell you how many people got up and walked out when he started in on religion. I thought it was hilarious and true. I hooked up with this married guy and we just fooled around for the rest of the trip. It was left in Vegas, never to be looked back on.

I was lonely and sad most of the time, wondering if I would ever be loved, feeling sorry for myself; still going out over and over again to fill the void. I decided to masturbate more and not have sex for a while. I actually loved to masturbate; I was guaranteed to get off. I loved to watch pornos to get me wet and use the toys I bought at the porno shop. If I didn't have the toys, I would use my hand. I was pretty obsessed with this. So often with one-night stands I never got off, and now I was getting off all the time and boy was I horny. After I would orgasm I would cry or feel really alone;

that was the hard part. There was no love with another body involved, I missed the closeness. I would tell myself I didn't have the closeness when a man was there either, so it really didn't matter.

I ran into an old high school friend who worked for a big company. I ended up producing a commercial for them. In the process he and I became friends again. He was married to a white girl with a few kids. He didn't seem to be all that happy. He and I were only friends; I never went down that road with him. We found out another high school friend was getting married in Colorado and we decided to travel together. Of course the wife knew nothing about it. When I say high school friends, I am not telling you the truth. We all just knew each other from a small school (really small). But, these people were never really friends; we just had Mattawan in common. So, my friend and I fly off to see a few old "friends" and the night before the wedding I go out and get all fucked up. I had never felt secure around these people and the drinking helped. I met up with Roy, this guy who was a few years older than me. In school we use to tease each other a lot, but we never hooked up. He was one of the few black guys at our school. I could name every black person there since it was so small. Anyway, he and I did our share of partying, but nothing

135

more until the wedding. He came back to the room I was sharing with my friend and we got it on in the bathroom; then we moved to the bed and proceeded to have sex right next to my friend as he snored. I have never heard someone snore so loud. Once Roy left I went and slept in the bathtub; the snoring was so loud.

After Colorado, I of course never heard from Roy again. He lived in Kalamazoo. I figured he was either married or involved. Didn't matter, I just moved on to the next.

The next was Larry from California. I met Larry through Dick and Sandy. Larry and I hooked up for dinner and we hit it off pretty well. Larry is a special effects guy in Los Angeles. He was a very talented artist and working in the film world, so we had a lot in common. He came by before he went home to LA and we ended up having sex. Different than most of my sexual encounters, this time it was sober. Larry was in the process of making an independent film and wanted my help. We kept in touch and when he was in town we would get together, but it was nothing more than that.

I awoke one night in terrible pain. I started to get chest pains and man were they painful. I couldn't do anything with them. I would wait it out and eventually it would go away. At some point I realized it was from too much wine... or too much rum and coke. That didn't seem to stop me from drinking though.

I took a trip to Florida to see my brother Robert. My parents and I went during the holiday. Robert was in a relationship with a real nice girl, but he was still really strange. He was now into energy, something I didn't know anything about. I remember him taking my rings, running his hands over them and coughing, saying the rings held a lot of negative energy and they needed to be cleansed. He also had this big pyramid over his bed to keep the negative energy out. He was always up and down with his drinking, one day he was sober, the next day he was drinking again. He has been labeled an alcoholic, and I guess you could say the same about me; I just never got that label and I never went to any class where I had to stand up and say it, nor would I. The trip was ok, how good can a trip be with Mom and Dad? I remember giving Robert $100 for Christmas and he just looked at it and said, "this it?" It was never good enough with Robert.

After being on the road forever with the parents I was more than happy to get home.

When I got home I found out that my friend's lover had kidney failure. He was in pretty bad shape and now he was being put on a donor list. I don't know if he ever got the kidney.

I was involved with Dick and Sandy doing this stupid music video show that was just a pilot. I was to shoot and edit the show, Sandy (of course) was the on camera talent and I'm not sure what Dick did. They introduced me to this guy named Ken; he was to be the money guy backing the show. I couldn't stand the pervert. We would go into bars to do interview stuff and all he wanted me to do was shoot the hot looking girls. I got so sick and tired of him telling me how to do my job; to top it off, I was doing it free! One night we set it up to go to this club and interview this band. In doing it I met Chuck. Chuck was the lead singer and about ten years older than me. After the interview he and I sat out in his car and talked for a long time. He called and we started going out. I was starting to really want more of a long-term relationship; I was tired of the one nighters and I was looking for something more stable. I thought I saw that in Chuck. I clung on to him. He was smart, had his own business, he was older, and he liked to have a good time; I really thought we had so much in common that we would for sure keep it going. Chuck unfortunately wasn't so good in bed. He was really rough and I never (until much later) had a good time in the sack with him. I faked it and faked it good. He tried so hard and I felt like I should give him at least a fake orgasm. Chuck would keep his distance from me if he felt like I was getting too needy.

I decided to spice it up and do up Valentines Day for him. In my mind I was thinking this would win him over: I cooked a wonderful meal, he came to the door, there was a blindfold on the door that he slipped on, he comes in and I took him into the bathroom. He took off the blindfold and I had a bottle of his favorite whiskey and a shot glass. I had candles burning and I had sexy underwear he had to put on. I put out a note saying when he comes out of the bathroom, to follow my heart. When he came out of the bathroom, I had red hearts laid out on the floor that he had to follow. In the living room he passed the TV, which was playing a porno. With another shot of whiskey, he came upstairs and entered the room where I am waiting. The room was completely filled with balloons, the bed was covered in pink satin and had a white screen draped over it like a tent, so

139

the balloons weren't in the way. I was lying there in this sheer robe, pink, with a sexy pink bra and undies. I had two video cameras set up and rolling and I served him strawberries, chocolate, whip cream and then we had this wild sex. This blew his mind and so much so that he dumped me. We never really had bad words with each other; he just didn't want a relationship and felt that he should end it before I got too carried away.

I started to do a gratitude journal to help me feel like I was actually grateful for this life and all of the things in it. I can't say that it ever worked, but I was loyal to writing in it for a while. When I read it now, it really kind of nauseates me. Here, let me show you why:

Today I am grateful for a lazy quiet day, also for simple laughter, grateful for consciousness, I am grateful today for a slow burn of the candle, for simple abundance. Feeling really good today, told another guy that I wasn't interested, I am following my heart, no more just to fill a void. This feels good, can you imagine the feeling of finding your spirit, life is beautiful. Good is all there is, evil is of the five senses.

Today I am grateful for a wonderful lunch with an old friend, for having

140

my hair shampooed, so grateful for a bookstore, for a challenging mind, to love this journey. I'm grateful for my wonderful parents, and all the love and positive feelings I am having. I'm slowly getting it! For today was a beautiful day.

Today I am grateful for my mom and her beautiful soul for the singing birds that bring joy, for taking a chance and trying something new and enlightening, running my own business, for living things, for life. My mom is coming up every two weeks to clean for me. I love having her here! Had another great day. One day closer to authenticity.

Puke!

Chapter Twelve

I did this video for my Mom and entered her in the Oprah Mom thing. I didn't get on Oprah, but Channel 3 honored my Mom. They came out and did an interview, which was really cool, and showed a piece of the video I produced. At first I really wanted to do a big thing with a video where everyone talked about how amazing and unconditional my mom is and then I wanted to send Mom and my dad to Hawaii. I couldn't afford it alone so I called some people to ask if they would donate whatever they could to make this trip possible and then I would pay the rest. I made the mistake of calling my uncle, my dad's brother. He thought it was ridiculous that I would stoop so low as to ask for money and told my dad, he said it was an embarrassment to the family. Then Dad called me and told me to call off the whole thing. "How does this look, you going around asking for money to send us to Hawaii?" "That's stupid and I won't allow it!" I was so pissed off; I swore to never involve the snobby, shallow Rothi side again. No one else seemed to have a problem with it, but the trip never happened because Dad made sure it didn't. At least I did get mom some appreciation in the channel 3 news report. I don't have many fond memories of my Dad's side of the family. My grandparents always favored my cousins over my brothers and I and it was really obvious. My Grandma was really religious. She never supported my singing because, she said, God gave me the voice and I should be singing for the church not in bars or in a band. My cousins were very snooty and I had nothing in common with them. I hated going to their house, didn't want anything to do with them. They were a very pretentious family that was all too proud!

One night when I was really depressed I wrote to Oprah again, this time it was about Andy and about me moving on. They actually called and wanted me to send them photos. I did all of this last minute, but for some reason (I can't remember why) they didn't use my story on the show and I got a T-shirt instead. I was thinking it was a show on women who had gotten through a hard divorce but then I thought the show was about women that were still not over the divorce years and years later!! Oh man, I sure didn't want to be on that show! Oh well, it was exciting in the moment. I wore that T-shirt until it fell apart. It felt good to just write and write what was bottled up, whether I got on the show or not. Someday, Oprah and I will meet; I always felt that, someday.

Ken, the guy backing the pilot that never took off, had asked me into his office for an appointment. This amazingly beautiful dog came wandering in; it was a Bernice Mountain dog. The owner came in after his dog and after I left he asked Ken for my phone number. When he called he made it all business like he wanted to talk about video. The truth is he wanted a date. I couldn't remember him and to be quite honest I wasn't at all attracted to him. On our first date though, he was quite funny and I found him charming. He always made himself out to be loaded and the topper was that he lived on a lake. I dreamed of living back on a lake and he mentioned renting out the downstairs. Bart didn't want to tell me his age but he finally did; he had just turned 50, which made him a good sixteen years older than me. I have never cared about age. As long as there was a connection, age didn't matter, younger or older. Younger actually bothered me a little. As you have read, I didn't go younger that much; the guys were almost always older. I was afraid I would get old first and the guy would leave me for someone younger, better to just avoid that.

Once Bart and I started we didn't stop until two years later. Most of my relationships lasted under two years; most of them never lasted longer than one night. I honestly can't remember one that was longer, until now. I think I was just tired and I wanted so much to settle down. I never wanted kids, but I needed someone to love me, someone I could count on and stay with for a while. When I look back, I knew this was a desperate attempt to make nothing into something. On about the second or third date Bart took me to this bar and at the same time scheduled a meeting. I felt like a showpiece and it really pissed me off. I got good and drunk and when I got home I went into the bathroom. When I came out he was gone. He couldn't even hack talking about it. I knew then. I ignored him for a while and he kept bugging me, so I let him back in to explain.

It wasn't long before I went to Detroit to meet his family. His mom had passed; his dad is an ornery old man, his brother is a drug addict, and his sister is a control freak with a husband that hit on me. What a nightmare, but I figured I wasn't dating the family, just Bart. Bart never wanted kids either; his reasons are totally different than mine, and one hundred percent selfish. I was dreaming a lot, but not sure what my dreams really meant. I had different takes on the dream state at this point; today if I look at my dreams I would say a deeper meaning was there, I just couldn't see it and once again was doing all I could to make the shoe fit.

Dream: Bart was first a total stranger, mean in the eyes, he is grabbing at my arm and hurting me saying mean things. I remember I couldn't believe it was Bart and how much he changed. I remember waking up and thanking God it was a dream. A whole series of dreams with people changing on me. My parents up and left me, cleaned out the house. I was on the phone crying, and they all of a sudden came back. It was strange, like my mom did it all. Then slowly it came out that my dad was in on it too. They arranged my marriage, at first I felt like my life was arranged, and they weren't my parents. Then it changed, they were just living made up lives in order to arrange a rich wedding. My mom was really a rude heavy drinker and my dad just out there for his own and all these people were in on it Andy's parents weren't religious at all, so hard to explain these dreams. They twisted into different people but represented mostly deceit. I remember they had to confess to me the big lie, and I was devastated. No one was who they appeared to be, starting with Bart and I felt like a good thing is now over. I tried to get out of the dream and realized I wasn't dreaming. I was crushed to think this man I loved turned so cold. It's 3:30 a.m and I just had to write this down, I will try to remember more later. It really is so hard to put what these dreams make me feel like on paper, lost, alone and younger. I remember telling Kim on the phone I wouldn't go to a foster home then they returned and told me all this stuff about my life being one big lie and that I did fall for Andy, and it hurts, but they didn't think I would get the divorce and that ruined their plans for me and their future. So they started being who they really are, so weird, I'm now going back to bed.

This might not make sense now, but keep reading, it will.

One thing that I was aware of was that I was growing spiritually and Bart didn't get any of it. He could talk the talk, but walking it was another story. For my birthday I wanted to go to Chicago to see Gary Zukav. I wanted Bart to open his mind some and take on a new thought. He agreed to go, but I knew he dreaded it. I am not the kind of person that is interested in workshops and lectures and all that crap. I really just didn't have any expectations and felt going couldn't hurt. The trip was a joke; Bart wanted to skip out on the classes and I can't say I blamed him. One of the first things Gary Zukav said was, "If you see me walking down the hall, leave me alone." I thought this was a bit rude, considering we are all supposed to be one. It wasn't a cheap deal either. All of the little exercises were stupid and we left feeling like we gained nothing. I had much to learn about spiritual masters, gurus and all that jazz in the years to follow. I must confess I went on a spiritual ride, just following what the masters were saying. I read everything, every book possible on self-help. I read all of Wayne Dyer's, all of Marianne Willimsons', Deepak Chopra, *Course In Miracles*, Stuart Wilde, Eckert Tolle, Don Miguel Ruiz, Jane Roberts, every different kind of religion. You name it and I read it; I was on a flow, or so I thought.

I can't remember how I got talked into moving in with Bart. I know the business was doing ok; maybe I thought I could save some money and get out of paying my big rent payment. Maybe I thought I would have some security, or I wanted to live on a lake again. We talked about it and I had been to his house a lot. He lived way out in Canonsburg on the other side of town. There was this cute little house for sale across from his house. This little cottage was not on the lake, but I thought it would make a great studio and if things didn't work out then I would have a place to stay. We agreed the cottage would be perfect since he didn't have any room for my business, my furniture or anything I had, even Schekki. I bought the cottage, Bart co-signed, and when I moved out of the apartment, he didn't lend a hand; I was on my own doing the move, except for good ol' Eddie who came through to help. Everything I owned went into the cottage, even Schekki. I knew I would spend everyday there working so Schekki would be fine. Bart didn't want anything to do with my cat; he had his cat Bill and his dog Maddie. I had a few things at Bart's house like clothes and bathroom stuff, that's really it.

The cottage was a great place to do business. I paid the house payment and very soon found out I had to pay more, much more. One night sitting on the couch, Bart said to me "its not what you do, it's what you don't do" and that would be not making as much money as him and never being his equal. He wanted me to start paying half of everything, even half of his mortgage. Bart had a very expensive lifestyle, which was a big joke to me. He was always out kissing everyone's ass to look important. We would go out for dinner and he would expect tit for tat, he could never just take me out without me returning the favor! My dad once said, "You might make some money if you would stop eating out so much." Bart always said, "Just write it off."

I drank every single day unless I was hung over. Bart always had to entertain or be entertained. He would travel all the time, he said for business, and I was really starting to forget everything I read. I was starting to lose it, getting more and more insecure which Bart loved reminding me of daily.

Something was always happening on the lake and soon after living there I found out that Bart slept with pretty much every woman on the lake. He still got together with a few of them but said they were just friends. It's important to Bart to always remain friends with every girl he has fucked, dated or whatever. He enjoys thinking that he is popular, cool and women like him. He flirted openly with women when I was around. He was always the first one into the party and when he's on, he's on. I could go all night without even seeing him. I could see all of this clearly and it made me sick, but I didn't know what to do. I was stuck! I just drank more, cried more, and got more depressed. I'm sure we must have had a few good times, but I honestly can't remember them.

Bart's dad was visiting and I hadn't been feeling good. I was 34, my tits were killing me, and I was tired and felt like puking. I decided I needed to take a pregnancy test. I remember taking the test and it reading positive, sitting alone in the bathroom. I was confused, emotional and I needed to tell Bart. I got him to come inside to tell him about my new found pregnancy and he was so cold to me. No question, you will have an abortion. That was it! I didn't want a kid, and I truly didn't want a kid from this asshole, but a little compassion would have been nice. He said he would pay half; yeah, half of everything that's how it goes. I really wanted him to go with me, I needed him there and once I scheduled the appointment he conveniently had to play golf. Mom ended up going with me and I was grateful for that. She never said a word; she just supported me. The abortion was quite painful and I cried all the way home. I'm not sure why. It just came pouring out. Mom stayed with me the whole day, Bart was nowhere to be found.

Bart decided he should get a vasectomy so he didn't have to go through my abortion again. I, though, went with him. I was there for him and he expected it. He pretty much demanded it.

Our first Christmas together was ok, busy since Bart had to entertain everyone. Robert came home from Florida with his girlfriend and that was nice to hang out with them. We got pretty fucked up in Detroit with Bart's family, doing coke, smoke and alcohol. I got so pissed off at Bart that I took off and walked and walked; he finally came looking for me. I really just wanted to get lost and to never be found. The next day I was hung over and we had to go to my parent's house. They never knew; I just went through the motions.

One of the funniest things that I remember was my Christmas present. Bart made such a big deal out of it and I couldn't imagine what it would be. He took me downstairs and there in all of its glory was a big drum set! A fucking drum set! I didn't even play the drums nor had I ever mentioned having an interest in drums. It was pretty obvious to me that they were for him, yet he said it was my Christmas present. Bart played keyboard and some guitar; once in awhile we would go downstairs and I would sing as he played. It was always a drunk night, but it was a release for me to be doing something with music. But a drum set? Are you kidding me! I ended up selling them and because Bart never paid the guy for the set, I agreed to give him half the money. It was my Christmas present after all.

It was getting pretty common that Bart and I were fighting all the time. I didn't trust Bart, never did. I found myself sleeping in the house across the street a lot. Schekki loved it. I hated it. I couldn't stand being that close to him. Then he would come over all drunk and beg me to come back.

He decided he wanted to take a trip to Costa Rica and take his dad and his brother. I could go, but I had to pay half. I thought this would be fun; I love to travel so I decided to go, I mean I was his so-called girlfriend…so called. I had the impression Bart had never been to Costa Rica so he did some research and thought the place was great and not that expensive.

The trip was a complete disaster. I learned more about Bart then I cared to know, his self centered ways. I even had a complete stranger say she would pray for me! It was all about Bart; Bart getting to the bottom of the waterfall before everyone else, Bart getting to the top first, Bart riding the horse better than anyone, Bart taking the ropes in the jungle faster and first. It was never ending, this selfish shit. I did see it before, always, but here in the jungle, you would think he would hold out a helping hand!

Let me tell you this before I go into more details: in Grand Rapids, he would never walk by my side it was always two steps ahead of me. He always entered every party first and he always criticized the way I dressed.

"Me", "me", "me", it was always Bart first, always! In Costa Rica it was no different! We did a day out in the rainforest and he said I didn't need tennis shoes. Well he failed to mention that he brought another woman to this exact same place (and he paid her way), that he knew exactly where we were going and that I indeed needed tennis shoes. I climbed all the way down to the bottom of this waterfall in my sandals. It was so hard; I was tore up big time from bugs for weeks after. Along with legs so sore that I could barley walk, I rode a horse that nearly bucked me off after seeing a coral snake on the path, I swung from ropes high up in the trees…all while wearing these sandals. Bart never once walked by my side, never once held out a helping hand! That night I got drunk. Bart was off somewhere and this local guy asked if I wanted to go see the monkeys, I agreed and off we went. Bart came around the corner to find me heading off into the woods to see the monkeys. He was so pissed off; he went off on this guy, picking up a big rock and throwing it right at the guy's head! I will never, ever forget this! He bent over wailing in pain as Bart grabbed my arm and dragged me back to the room. Oh, now he gives a shit!

Ken and Bart ended up getting some killer weed and Ken wanted to bring it back into the States. That was crazy, but he pulled it off! The trip was a joke, Bart was a joke; shit, his family was a joke and I just wanted to get free! I took a scuba class in Costa Rica and I just didn't feel right about any of it. Bart of course does everything, so I felt like I had to go through with it. They dumped me in the ocean and I just couldn't do it! Before we left, Bart had cosmetic eye surgery so he couldn't do the water. He was really embarrassed by me and insisted I learn how to dive so we could dive together at some point! I actually took diving lessons when I got back into Grand Rapids; I passed and I still don't like it. It's creepy to me to be way down in the water. I just feel it's not our place, not our world and we just need to leave things alone.

Chapter Thirteen

Not quite sure how to understand this. We were in a restaurant. I walk in on Bart and two men, and some people in the corner. One guy was sucking his dick, and he was kissing the other. I thought all this time that he is gay. I remember calling my mom crying and saying the wedding is off, he is gay. I kept talking and talking about it. I remember thinking I was going to tell everyone. It's like this dream is saying; I need to stop analyzing the relationship, stop talking about it. No matter where Bart is, it is over, the scene of the sex was the hardest. I swear it was the same dream over and over, the look on his face alone. The people all around.

One time on a trip to New York to meet Bart's best friend, when we got off the plane and he greeted his friend they kissed on the lips. I couldn't get that image out of my head. He was so infatuated by this guy. Always following after him. He decorated just like him, dressed like him, acted like him. It was creepy. The mind holds on to things and it can replay them at any time, even if you think you have forgotten it. With a dream it replays it in it's own way. There is no control on how the dream gets put together; it's chaos. I actually thought if Bart and I got married, things would work out. I actually asked him to marry me! I'm happy to say he turned me down! I tried and tried to figure it out, but there was nothing to figure out. I was learning that if I wanted to change him, maybe I needed to get out of the relationship!

One night Bart wanted to go to a concert without me, this was typical. I sat up half the night waiting for him to get home. Around 3am he showed up all drunk. I was so pissed off. I had a hunch he had been fucking around and I knew he had that night as well. We got into an actual fight, not only verbal. I decided since he had kept me up half the night wondering what he was doing that I would keep him up. So, I turned up the TV really loud and kept going at him verbally. He was so trashed that when he went to swing at me he missed. We had a small punching match that I was winning then he threw me up against the wall and down we went in a scramble. I thought the whole thing was pathetic, so I grabbed my pillow and headed across the street. The next day he was over at my house begging and pleading, saying he was sorry! I was so over him, but I still didn't know what to do or where to go! I gave it a couple days and went back again.

I really hated waking up at Bart's. The truth was I was just fine alone at the house across the street; it was just to close for me to actually move on from Bart. When I left him, I ate less, drank less, and smoked less! I started to walk and meditate; I knew I needed to get myself grounded. I started learning massage, reading more on energy and the chakra system. When I would cower and go back to him, I was back in the messed up mind set. I would wake to him watching the news, which I can't stand! I love to wake up slowly; take time to remember my dreams, take in the morning. Not Bart, and he could care less what I wanted. He wouldn't even compromise.

This time when I came back I told Bart that Schekki had to be included! I hated leaving him across the street and I wanted him with me more. He agreed, but wasn't at all happy about it. Schekki never liked Bart, and he would go downstairs and pee only on his stuff. I can't say I blame Schekki. Not too long after Schekki was moved in, Bart demanded he be caged when we were gone, and at night. His cat of course was free to roam. Maddie (the dog) and Bill (the cat) actually got along great with Schekki. It was Bart that didn't want Schekki around. I was so miserable about this, but it was his home and I didn't know what else to do. I was working on making my way out of this nightmare of a relationship. After the millionth time that I moved back, and all of his promises that he would never keep, I knew I had to start manifesting my freedom. I met this guy Don that owned a business. He was primarily a Disc Jockey, but rented this building and wanted to bring in other wedding vendors. He offered me office space for $500 a month; I knew this was my out, at least for my business. I had to get the business out of the house across the street, and then figure out what I would do with me. I knew this would set me back a few bucks, but business was doing good and Don was sure I would do even better being in a storefront. I took his offer and moved the business. The house across the street was now sitting empty so I decided to rent it out to pay the mortgage until I could sell it. Bart at one time did a re-finance on the mortgage that I agreed to help him out with monetarily; I thought I would get some of it, but he got $10,000 and I never got a penny. I did get a higher monthly payment that I continued to struggle with.

One day I came home; it was raining and cold outside and I saw Schekki's cage thrown out the front door. The cage was lying on its side and the door was open. Schekki was gone! I was hysterical! Bart threw him out and now Schekki was gone. Days went by; I searched and searched for him, standing on the deck calling for him, crying. Bart thought I was ridiculous and I could give a shit what he thought! I was standing on the deck and I could hear this faint cry; it was so quiet, but I heard him. Schekki was curled up in a ball under the deck. I'm sure that's where he must have been the entire time. I was pissed at Bart. I knew Schekki was not safe and I felt horrible for how he was being treated. I decided to ask Mandy and Brian if they could take him for a while until I figured out my living space. They did. And I cried!

I said in my dream, "I'm afraid I might die now" and he responded, It's going to happen. Not sure exactly how he said it. Yet, I remember it hitting me like you are going to die. No fear. If I live, I experienced one more thing, if I die; I died experiencing one more thing. To live in fear is your own death.

I was dreaming like crazy these days, I have books and books of dreams. I really didn't understand the dream state. I often thought you had insights to your waking life; other times it was nothing more than a carry over from your day or days before. I was really into death, fear and what was real. I would say to Bart none of it's real anyway, and he would just get all pissed and say, " What the fuck are you talking about, of course it's real." That's not what I meant! A deep conversation with him was about non-existent!

I met this couple that lived across the lake and the guy played in a band. I ended up joining the band for a short time, singing. We never made it out of the practice room but it was fun while it lasted. Bart was so negative on everything I did; I was defeated and left the band. I think he was happy knowing I was sitting at home waiting for him. Was I happy? It really didn't matter!

Quite irritable today, the little things are really getting to me. Selfish prick and loving that "do unto me and only me." I think of helping no one, unless it helps me. No it's not my motto. It sure holds true for people I know. I have been waiting to get this information in the mail from Marywood, spiritual information. I'm ready to let go what I can't control, to let people be, find myself and be!

I can't remember how I met this girl! All I can remember is her telling me about this school for spiritual formation and that she was getting out of Michigan. She said the energy was really low and needed to go somewhere more open. I decided to investigate this class. It really excited me and I asked to get more information. I enrolled and was accepted! I was surrounded by such negative people; I really needed to expand my consciousness and be open to other things! I was meeting people that were like-minded and they were introducing me to new things. Bart thought I was getting a little snobby with this newfound freedom. I guess he'd do anything to hold me back. I didn't let it happen this time though. I also went to a reader, one for past life regression! It was really a great experience for me. She said Bart was temporary; I would find my door, open it, then close it! She mentioned Gramps, which was hard for me! It was good; Bart of course said it was all a bunch of shit. That I would believe her and ruin such a "wonderful" relationship!

Loose paper writings -

Do me a favor and live the next week of your life without me in it! You go your way and play your games. I on the other hand have a different road to take. It's been fun, I must say, but things are changing and the distance is clear, I won't live a life based on fear. Be your own person and live as you may, my presence here is not welcome, that's clear. I have much to do and times are wasting in this drama with you! Give and take it's so simple to do, to find laughter in all that you do, you choose different than what I want to do. I'm tired of this worry of pleasing you! If it works and it's true, God bless this life when it's through!

Why you demand so much from me can't seem to please him when it comes from the depth of me. I give up this and give up that only to hear, it's not enough! Who can say what is real? I'm down on my knees, begging please. This life of mine is not, I let others control my thought. I want to be free to live and love to conquer this world and move above. Let no walls be in place, There are no limitations in this place. We tend to believe what we are told, boundaries, that are sold, give me a break is what I say, what can you do to turn my heart away? This is life here and now, lost and confused yet surviving somehow! I can do it in this life, make my way, and silently part. I love my Bart with all I can, when it's too much I bless and go on and on and on. Thirty six I confess, could you get that with a guess? Much to do and to see, limitations are nothing but debris. What is shall be and I will see God is always with me.

It's not working, what can I say? I tried everything and it's not here to stay. Do the dishes, laundry, care for my cat, empty the garbage and see to that! Care for me, do it now! I took you in, I own you now! Cook my dinner, change the sheets, kiss my ass in this heat, do for me and your approved. Open the door turn on the heat change the litter box, Oh, you're way too sweet! Bring me a drink is all I ask now bend over and kiss my ass! When will you be what I want you to be? You avoid my direction and you're not listening to me, you have nothing without me. I'm your all, bow down to me! I called and you weren't there, needing a friend and someone to share. Same old story, same old dance just need you to listen and take that chance. The guess is true, and you not knowing when you loose. It's better I must say to be alone. No one to answer, not even the phone. You do as you please, be happy in it, I miss that freedom that I once was in it! Here I am what's wrong now, the way I dress? The composure I hold? What would you change if you could? My attitude or my obedience with you? Being me is hard for you. The lie we live is hard to do, you don't love me and I don't love you!

Hi, my name is Bart; let me impress you with my past, because I have no future! Cater to me, take care of me, whim to my needs, you have none. Me and me alone, needs. I wake up and smell what I need for me. You did what? Oh well, I am self-sufficient. Up and down, all around. Oh, you talked and yet I don't approve, fuck me. It's not right, I am governed. I know what's right and you're not it! How fucking dare you. You have a mind of your own? Do unto me as I would do unto me, get out!

Aggression is great! And that is what I'm doing. I right now hate this man, no questions? No excuse? He plays his fucking games, and I should just allow, isn't that what women do? Not I! I no straight up, good fucking luck! Godspeed and all that shit!

I let my mind take me away, floating in space -- this is my destiny -- freedom from pain and anguish so true. I live my life for what's true. Down from earth you fall and see my heart and I must feel empty. What are dreams here for -- I get drunk, all alone. You leave me here laughing and laughing. Take your laughter and your tears, go somewhere else with your fears. I am lost within this game. I hate you, just the same. You're an asshole, because you know what you stole. It's over. Goodbye my friend.

Chapter Fourteen

Dream

I was afraid, I remember jumping back as though I was going to be hit. Then we were at a bar. It was heaven for a while and I felt fear. I sense that I was sexually abused then the person turned out to be Bart and I felt embarrassed and sick to my stomach. He was yelling things to these two lesbians and asked for a three some. I got up went to the bar and said, I can't eat, this food is awful, this man is an ass and I got to go. I felt as though I was sneaking out so he wouldn't hold me down and hurt me more. I got out and it was raining, pouring and I'd ditched behind some building and saw a bunch of firemen. I ran and asked for their help. I said, I went to Mattawan, I'm Schelli Rothi. Will you help a friend, and they were more than willing to take me to safety. I reflected back and thought I just left home all alone and realized he went home with the two lesbians. I awoke this morning feeling afraid feeling hate and jumpy, that fear of someone slapping you and you jerk back. Good morning, love, have a beautiful day and heed the warning.

I was doing all I could to make things work between Bart and I, and since the cottage was just sitting I finally found these guys to rent it. They were a bit shady and Bart didn't like them, but he wasn't paying the mortgage… it was my call! I decided to see past their wild ways and give them a shout! It was this Andy guy and his brother. I left everything of mine in the house, all of my furniture, dishes, towels; everything for them to use, even my bed and sheets! Oh, and not to mention my beautiful new oak table. See, my stuff was never good enough in Bart's eyes, so my "brand new" furniture was left there! These guys were set and I was cool about it all! Pay the rent on time and there will be no credit checks, no nothing! Just pay the fucking rent! I was more than patient with the whole thing. It was always cash and I was fine with that, but not a month went by when I didn't have to go begging for my money. This started to wear on me! I'm not good at confrontation. I feel if you just handle it, everything will be fine; no need to argue! They really were pushing my buttons though and underneath it all I was ready to explode!

I had Bart riding my ass about them being teenage wild boys, and there I was doing what I could to keep the peace! Maddie started to go into heat and Bart wanted to breed her. I mean after all she was worth thousands of dollars, her puppies anyway! This whole breeding thing really bugs me. I don't support any of it and want no part of it! One night Maddie went out wandering, she always did, but being in heat was a different kind of wandering. She was looking to get laid! Bart was out again and I knew I was fucked if I didn't find her! I set out and searched for her. I ended up finding her up at this woman's house (across a very busy road)! Maddie was locked down with this pit bull! I was freaking out. Bart had already found her a mate and now she was totally getting laid, and by a pit bull! I just started laughing and laughing; I have never seen two dogs get locked down like that. I guess once the male puts his penis in it swells so much that they are stuck like that for a long time and you don't even want to think about separating them! Once the whole thing was over I took Maddie home and broke the news to Dad! He was irate, blaming me for everything and that she better not be pregnant by this pit bull! Okay, do I really need to explain how fucked up this is? He ended up taking her for a pregnancy test and, well, she wasn't pregnant. Hey Bart, looks like you can profit off of your loving pet after all! The funny thing about this story to me is I didn't support this whole thing, not one bit! As a matter of fact, the owning of any animal is fucked up to me! Mary (my neighbor) and I had to take Maddie to her bought lover about five hours away. We did the drive and I will never forget watching Maddie with the other Bernice and how she hated being there; she kept running away with her tail between her legs. Maddie kept looking at me, like, please don't leave me here! I had no choice but to walk away and leave her there to get impregnated! I felt horrible and so did Mary! The thing is Maddie never got pregnant from this dog either or any other dog Bart set her up with. All the money he put out to get his money puppies, they never happened! That is funny to me!

My friend Larry from California ended up producing his film. I ended up going to LA for the first time to shoot for him. I of course was a no body, just there to help, with no dollar signs attached to my ass! Bart wasn't too concerned about me going. He was happy to have me gone so he could have his alone time with his girlfriends. I knew I had to go; I had to just check it out! Bart never knew Larry and I had slept together. I honestly don't think he would have cared anyway; it would have just justified his seeing all of his past lovers. The LA trip was fine, busy! Larry and I were platonic as we had been since I hooked up with Bart. We did the movie out in the desert, in this small town that I really liked. I did as much as I could to help out Larry; I drove the big ass camper up to location all by myself. Whatever he asked I would do. I'm a helper, and when the trucks came with the gear I jumped in to help unload, but was quickly removed because in LA you have this union shit. Everyone has a job title and to go beyond that is just wrong! I learned that right away. The best part was doing a shot on the train. They tied me down to the edge of the train and I shot the car race from below, which was cool. We had a major dust storm one night and, well, the end of the shoot was the best! Larry had a car scene where the car fell off a cliff. I loved that part, I had one camera set up on a ladder then once the other car hit the main car I got off the ladder and ran to the edge to get the full crash of the car coming down the mountain! It was so exhilarating! I really did have fun. I met a guy who I liked a lot, but my loyalty to Bart was too strong; stupid me! I did know that I had no interest living in LA! Too busy and too much drama for me! Too competitive as well! But I was always grateful to Larry for putting me on the film! His film did Okay. He played at a lot of festivals; one festival in Muskegon that I went to. Outside of that, I have no idea what became of the film.

Not sure what it is. I've had a strong feeling to write and I don't know why. I'm feeling lost, I struggle for words. Things have been coming to me, visions and clarity and understanding and knowledge on how simple everything is and why we tend to make everything so difficult. We create these intense struggles in our lives. We live by rules and who is to say how we should live our lives? Who really has the answers? We do, we just need to listen and be true to ourselves and not to take things so serious. Life can be that cut and dry. Don't think so hard. Let things be, don't blame yet do for yourself. Do not change and allow, it is death, for we are forever evolving. Choice, that is ours. We can live consciously or shut down and try to control everything and complain when things don't go as we think they should or understand and learn and experience. Live in this human body and experience, don't just believe what someone else says it should be, there are no coincidences. Know your experience; don't stand on the outside waiting to be let in. Do it for the fun and adventure of it. What could it hurt? We are all going to die, but that's the physical. Don't waste it now. We have many lives, but you don't know that, you think this is it -- nothing more, what a sad existence. You're so shallow -- but if you really thought that this is your only chance than why not want to give it your best -- what do you have to lose? And if you choose to realize there is so much more than the human experience then you already know. You just know! So laugh, love, dance and sing. Live your authentic life and

171

don't take things so serious. After all, we've created it! Do what you need to do in this life and that is all that matters. You'll see!

Bart decided he needed to do something to make himself feel like a good guy, so he wanted to be a big brother! I found this thing hilarious! It was all one big lie anyway! I had to disappear because it wouldn't look good having me there. The kid was his quest to feel better about himself; it was shallow and sad. Once again I wanted no part of his bullshit! The kid became his excuse to not be home and soon I realized it was just that! Outside of me doing all I could to keep it together, the relationship was pretty much done!

There were always parties on the lake, we went to all of them and fought after every one. Our neighbors had one, but this one was really out there; this is the one that put an end to it all. Not once did Bart ever hang with me at a party. He went off on his own and this one was no different. Of course I already knew he had slept with every woman on the lake and I had come to terms with that. I had enough! I was done with it all. This time, for what I can remember this guy was really coming on to me. I wasn't comfortable with it, yet a part of me felt like Bart needed a slap in the face. It really didn't matter, he had disappeared with another girl and I was so drunk that I decided to just leave. I stumbled back to the house. Halfway home I lost my footing and fell down some stairs. I wandered over to this bush and I remember trying to keep it together, then I just fell flat on my face. I woke up in the bushes and hours later I stumbled home, broke down the door and crashed. I woke up to a bed full of leaves! One day Mandy and Brian were bringing Schekki home; Brian had an allergy and couldn't take it anymore. I talked to Mandy and she and I did a walk to see where I fell. This guy came out of the house and said, "Are you looking for a bracelet?" I fell into this guy's bush and woke up to third degree burns on my hand from my cigarette! I didn't remember anything and I was devastated! I couldn't go on like this! Something had to change!

After this, I ended up moving downstairs for the remainder of my days with Bart. It was horrible trying to get through each day. I met some great people, Shawn and Melissa. Shawn was so kind as to say, "You gotta get out, you can live with us until you find a place." I jumped on it!

Dream: there was one in front of me and one behind and we were at the top of the slope. I was scared to death, watching the first person right on the edge and yet feeling very comfortable. I was next, and I let the person behind me go first. I had someone guiding me telling me to go for it, have no fear. I looked down the hill, and just couldn't do it. It was steep, and I wasn't comfortable I said. "I thought we were diving today, not skiing." I never did it -- I chickened out.

I was living with Bart (downstairs), my business was on West River Drive and I was surviving. I had a pretty good relationship with the couple where I had my business. When walk-ins came in, they would recommend me and I was booking. Business was doing pretty good. I wasn't getting the high-end weddings I wanted, just a lot of low-end weddings, but a job was a job and I never turned it down. The little ones added up. Eventually I introduced Shawn, who I thought was a really outgoing guy that would be a great DJ, to the guy that ran this business. He was working at the post office but had some political issues and was on a layoff. They didn't hit it off at all. As a matter of fact after much fighting Shawn left and said, "Get out as soon as you can." This wasn't the first time I heard that! I knew there was some weird shit going on, but it really didn't affect me, so I kept on.

I was walking outside of my house when I heard cars squealing around the corner, I sat back and watched as this car came speeding up then halted across the street from my house followed by five police cars! Ok, now what? From what I hear, the guys that were renting the cottage from me had run from the cops and were followed. The cops believed there was a meth lab in the house. They never got in without a warrant and soon I discovered Andy had split. I was dealing with the other guys. I found out that, unknown to me, many guys are shacking up there. This one guy was pretty good about it all. It was a mess; Andy (the rent payer) left, which meant no rent. The other guys were just trying to figure out what they were going to do. I ended up getting them out with some nice talk. I got some cash, but not much and they left with a huge, fucked up mess to follow.

I left Bart and moved in with Shawn and Mel. Bart was a complete ass when I moved! At one point I did a long form production for this hot tub company and got a free hot tub. It was set up at Bart's house and he thought it was his! I made sure, come hell or high water, to take that with me! He was really a dick about me leaving, but I finally did it; I left and it felt so good! The cottage was a different story; he had some kind of interest. I'm not sure what it was honestly, but I did know I had an upper hand with the cottage! The renters destroyed the place, not to mention my furniture! The couch was ripped and torn, the oak table had a big scratch down the middle of it and the rest well, it's not worth the detail. It was a fucked up mess!

I wanted to sell the cottage and Bart wanted his piece of the pie. Now mind you, I paid all the payments, let him refinance and get all of that money, and he paid nada! He was just a co-signer and he wanted the sale on the house! I was done lying down, done giving it up. Not this time! Not ever again! And he knew it!

I want to go into this relationship a bit more. Since I was older you would think I would have known better. Before I met Bart I was starting to understand who I was. I was reading and experiencing life on a more spiritual level. I was still a very lonely person and still wanted so badly to find love. Most of us believe that love is with conditions. That we have to work at things and we often try so hard to do whatever we can to fit in and be accepted no matter what we have to give up. I still didn't have a clear understanding on this feeling of love nor did I understand who I was.

From the beginning things were not good. Bart was all about impressions and lies and I couldn't see this at first. He was funny and I did like his company at first and I was more than happy to move in with him since he was living on a lake and it appeared to me that he had money. I thought he would help me out. My business was doing well in that townhouse, I was doing well and a small part of me knew I shouldn't move in with him yet I still did. The move of course was a clue when he wouldn't even help me do that. I made the move anyway and buying that cottage across the street was one of the better choices I made.

When I made the move none of my things were allowed into his house, I had to put everything into the cottage across the street and this included Schekki. Bart had a dog, Maddie and a cat, Bill. He had no interest in my cat or my things. It was Bart's world and I had to try to fit in. Bart was a big drinker and pot smoker he enjoyed his cocaine as well. What I feel now is that he just wanted a prize, a younger girl to showoff. He also wanted me to cook, clean and be available. I had to pay rent to him too and half the utilities. We never spoke of these things before I moved in and it was quite a surprise when it came out. I would have been better off staying in the townhouse, but of course that's not how it happened.

Bart was more mentally cruel to me than anything. He liked what I did for a living since I could do video work for him for free. Besides that he never supported my business. Bart was an "on" kind of guy, always impressing the woman and talking his big stories. This really annoyed me. Communication was a joke; he never wanted to talk about anything unless it was money and getting more. I would always reach out to talk about higher energy things and he just didn't get it. All the books I read were very powerful to me, maybe it was the books that got me through two years.

Anyway, there were many stories in this relationship, many lies. He always had to have parties and invite people to show off to. He always invited all the women that he was in relationships with in the past and I am pretty sure during our relationship he hooked up with quite a few of these women. I was a very insecure woman and this never helped. He denied it always and told me to get over it, he never would try to work it through with me. I know he slept with most of the women on the lake and beyond. I was constantly being faced with all these women and I was really losing it! Cheating to me is interesting. If you want to cheat why not just end the relationship with the one you're with and move on. It's really so simple. If it isn't happening then MOVE ON!

Not Bart, he wanted his cake and he ate it too! I was living across the street probably more than living with him. We fought endlessly and he just avoided it at all costs. I honestly didn't know what to do, I felt as though I moved my whole world there and I was so far in debt I couldn't get out. I would stay in the cottage across the street and watch him bring women in and out of his house. When he was out of women he would come crawling back and want to work it out. I always gave in and went back, but nothing ever did change and I believe I started to realize that you couldn't change people; it just doesn't work that way and I realized it was me that needed to change and really get out!

Shawn and Mel were great friends and Shawn really felt I needed to get out as well. He and Mel offered for me to come live with them. This was my out and I went for it!

Bart served a purpose in my life. I really believe that he was my breaking point. What he said and did to me really was a turning point in my life with men and relationships. No one, and I don't care who you are, should ever put up with any abuse, physical or mental! Mentally I was drained in this relationship. I gave up on me and I believed everything he said about me. I was drunk half of the time to escape and I just felt sorry for myself. When I snapped, I really snapped! I started getting physical. Started walking everyday, then that turned into running. I started to go to the gym and I started to love myself. I dropped at ton of weight and started feeling good about me and I got free! I got out!

Chapter Fifteen

Living with Shawn and Mel was really nice, but they were a young couple planning to get married and I didn't want to intrude for long. I was still too close to Bart and when I drank I would miss him. When I sobered up, I got over it! The spiritual formation classes were good for me at this point in my life. I was still heavily involved with finding out who I was, trying to work through it all. The following is a letter I was asked to write, a letter about who I am, or more like how I was programmed.

When I was a child I was told that we were sin, heaven and hell. I would burn in hell if I was bad, that was sin. Young ladies should act a certain way. No wonder no one likes me by the way I act. I was told what my limitations were, I should get a decent job and stay there and retire and put money aside, get married, have kids, find security. My mom was good to me, living my dream -- do whatever I want yet afraid/fear. I was told that girls should always be quiet, stay in their place, dress and look pretty, be agreeable: stay away from boys, they are trouble, be polite. No burping or farting. Boys, that's a boy for you. I didn't fit the image always, I struggled to be outgoing, been criticized for it. Then I would try

181

to be like I was told and feel sad because that didn't work either. I believe that a woman should always just be, feel what she feels, just to be. The same for a man. I was told I should be on time, dress nice, do my hair, be thin, to make money and count on no one. Take care of myself! I believe I am beautiful. I am physical and happy. I smile and am good with people. I want to give and fix the problems. I am spontaneous and quiet. I am light and energy, and I am forever changing. I believe others think I try too hard, insecure, yet secure to others, strong personality, bossy at times, I want to make things all good. This is hard because so many people look at me differently. I hear humble and independent, I hear selfish and scared. I hear positive and happy. So many different things. I wish I could get stuff out of my head -- stop analyzing and trying to figure people out. To stop looking at the past or the future to stand taller with what I know! Not get sucked into drama and judgment to just allow and take nothing personal. My image of perfection that would be to feel beautiful to take better care of my body to have my business flowing so the money can take me where ever, to not have to think about that ever, to help others to laugh and love and live with no worry to fall into spiritual love, unconditional love, to be alive in every moment.

I found a condo in Grandville that I ended up buying, a cute place right on a lake. I moved out of Shawn and Mel's and started my new single life. I took my business out of that store front building and moved it back to my condo. The guy was not happy about this at all, but I knew it was something I had to do. He took the move very personal and even though I felt I had handled it well, he really did a number on my business. The details are a bit blurry and I guess I don't feel like going into it. It's done and I moved on, slowly. Business was down and I was very restless. I was filling my days with whatever work I could get my hands on that would help pay the bills. If I had too much alone time I would get depressed and miss the companionship with Bart. He would call often to try and get back together. I knew in my heart this would never happen; yet I felt sorry for him. I was still running and working out everyday. I started getting up at 5am every morning. I took on doing massage therapy in my condo and I also found making candles was fun. I was still going to my spiritual classes and I also took a part time job at a health store. I was staying busy and that was the point.

Steve had been working for me a while and I ended up bringing him into the condo to help with my business. When I worked at the health store I befriended this guy Justin. He had just broken up with his girlfriend and needed a place to stay, so I let him crash at my place. I thought I was living alone, but that's not true. I did everything I could to keep entertained, to not have to be alone and feel alone. I felt like I was so together doing all of these different things, so spiritual, so insightful; what a joke huh?

I got a call from Bart that Maddie had been hit by a car. I was devastated! Sweet Maddie, dead! I made a candle for Bart and went over to see him. That night we ended up getting together, and that would be the last time I would ever see Bart. Hear from him, yes; see him, no! I felt like shit bringing myself down to that level, knowing I was just filling a void. I knew it was over. I talked with Bart because we were trying to settle on the cottage across the street. He was a complete ass on the whole deal and I wasn't going to budge. I wanted $15,000 and then I would be out! He fought and fought with me on this but eventually knew he had no choice. I got the $15,000 and that was the end of it!

I loved my new home. I loved waking up to the water outside my window. I was really into meditation and stillness at this point in my life, finding my center. I was reading about decorating the house Feng Shui; I just loved the idea that I could do whatever I wanted with this place, and I did. Upstairs, in one of the rooms facing the cul-de-sac, is where I put my company (all of the editing equipment). I painted the room light purple and painted phrases all over the room like "the truth will set you free" and some other ones I ran across in my readings. I wasn't a believer in the God theory anymore. I was more on the "energy" and the "higher power" and "we are all connected" stuff. I didn't watch TV anymore so the living room was all re-painted with some really cool colors; the furniture was set up to look out the big bay windows. Downstairs I had to cut an area off to do my massage work. This was painted in a deep red, with screens up to block off my bedroom. I had soft music playing, usually Enya, and I worked with oils. I actually started making my own oils. I did pretty well with building a clientele for massage; they came from the gym or from working at the health store. I enjoyed doing massage. It was very rewarding. I was self-taught; I picked up some books and practiced, but most important my heart was into it. I started by working on friends and I never charged. Then when I started doing more I just asked for a donation. Massage to me is not a mechanical thing, it's about feeling and being in touch with the body. It's not about time; it's letting all of that go and being totally immersed in the moment! On the other side of the massage area was my bedroom. I wanted my room downstairs, facing out to the lake. I painted this room a light green. I just loved all of the colors, and had fun doing whatever I wanted. There was no right way or wrong way, just having fun playing with different ideas.

Being so active in so many different things I had no problem meeting men and "young men". I was shooting a gig at a bar for some stupid bikini contest (the things I do to keep the business going). I met this young guy Curtis. He followed me around and had some kind of interest in me, not sure what it was to be honest. Maybe he was off on older women, not sure, but he was too hard to resist. He was 21 and I was 37. We had a lot of fun together. He was a shy, very philosophical guy and I really enjoyed our conversations. I knew it was nothing more than that and I am sure he did too, but with the time we had we did enjoy each other. Eventually he just drifted away. I re-kindled my sex relationship with Chuck. Remember Chuck? I had changed so much and wasn't into any kind of long-term thing anymore. I just wanted to get laid! Chuck and I had sex a lot back before Bart and I never did have an orgasm, but this time around I was able to let go and enjoy the experience; I was able to start enjoying sex with Chuck. Chuck was always a bit wild sexually, he liked to dominate and control and once I allowed that it went just fine. If I wanted sensual sex, I would have to go elsewhere. Chuck was also a good friend, it was just that though and I finally got it.

Once I was all settled into my new place I threw a party. It went well; I of course got trashed and depressed. Chuck stayed with me for quite a while but once he left, I just got more depressed. I am 37 and I am alone. Yet I would try to convince myself that I was never alone, I was loved. That mindset didn't work all the time. There were times when I had to go out and see how much love I could get. I wasn't at all looking for a relationship; I just needed some attention and I knew I would get it at the bars. I loved to just go and talk to these different guys. All of the bullshit that would come out of their mouths; I was feeling like an expert in the single world and I wanted to write about it. I never did of course. It was all just shallow, desperate conversations and I was no different. I thought I was different though. I figured with all of these classes, my weight loss, and books that I was pretty enlightened. Oh, let me laugh out loud! I couldn't see that I was not any different. I was caught in this mind fuck of being loved and getting attention, then being alone and staying far away. I was a mess, still!

As I sat in the hot tub and watched the steam floating on top of the water and drifting and covering me, it billowed up to my face. It was thick yet, as it passed through me, all I felt was a slight mist resting upon me. I breathe deep and absorb the warmth that was for me. I look up to the moon and see and feel so many different dimensions, rays are searing out so bright. They fade and I see deep shadows drifting across the night. I listen and the rays move in and reflect down on the beautiful open water in front of me. I look upon the lake and follow the reflections, it presents flickering lights. I follow it up and see a two-story house with all its lights illuminating out over the lake and one light ever so bold, which is a television! I think, I've seen this reflection often, how and why would anyone choose television over the beauty of this night? I wondered who they were, what mattered to them, what passions they have, wondered if that was life to them and thought, I know me better than anyone, I want to know someone as well as I know me. I realized this is God, not a person, a form a human male or female. It is the all, the everything everywhere all the time, and it is love. It explodes love, truth, goodness, joy, warmth.

188

It is never ending and it's all ours!

I woke up around 2 a.m. with chest pains. My body is talking. I still have been drinking every day, wine and beer; always something. Why I feel the need to hold on to that?

It's funny, the things we do when we feel alone. I would dig back in my past to the guys I left behind and look them up. Of course it never went anywhere, but it felt good trying at least. I was so into dreaming at this point that if something came to me in my dream I would take it serious and act upon it. For example if I dreamed of an old love, then the next day I would call him up to make sure he was ok. If I dreamed of Schekki getting attacked by dogs, I wouldn't let him outside for a long time. There were times when my dreams did manifest in life, weird things that really didn't mean anything. One night I dreamed of Ted, my old boss at the cable company, and in the dream he had introduced me to his two daughters. His hands looked really big, and he looked so sad in the dream. That very day I ran into him at Sams Club and sure enough he introduced me to his two daughters; his hands were big and yes, he looked sad! What does it mean? Nothing really!

I decided to throw a New Years Eve party for the new 2003. I had just gotten back from Florida; I went to visit my parents and also to settle up on my debt with my dad. When I bought the condo, I borrowed $15,000 from my dad and I came up with the rest. Business was really crappy right about now and all of the little things I was doing were just not paying the bills. I was behind on everything and I mean everything! I had the $15,000 from the cottage with Bart and intended to pay Dad back with this money but I found myself needing another loan. I knew I had to present the money to him then ask for some of it back. So, I went to Florida to have him help me figure out my bills, which he did. We went through everything together and he gave me back exactly what I needed to catch up on all of my bills. Then I was back in debt with him for another $6,000. In the moment it worked, but I still wasn't bringing in any money so I just fell back into debt. I thought a party was a great idea. I was always really good about appearing to have my shit together! I didn't get drunk at this party, I had a good buzz on but outside of that I was pretty aware of what was going on. Quite a few people showed up and many never left. Mandy and Eddie got pretty fucked up. Mandy's husband Brian was sober. Mandy and I were having a good time dancing and messing around; just girl stuff, trying to get the guys excited. Kissing a little here and there.

Brian was really into it, he would have loved to watch us get it on. Eddie was into it as well, of course. We were all going to hop into the hot tub, Eddie was already in, when Brian started egging Mandy on to lift my top and suck on my tits. At this point I had enough and stopped everything and went to bed. I was letting Brian and Mandy use the downstairs while I pulled the sleeper sofa out for myself upstairs. After I went to bed I didn't know what went down until I got up in the morning to Brian and Eddie playing cards at the kitchen counter. Mandy was totally hung over and really sick. After they left, Eddie filled me in that he and Mandy fucked while Brian sat on the edge of the bed and watched! I was actually glad to hear it! Glad to hear Mandy fucked another guy! Why? I don't know really. I was just glad.

I signed up to run a marathon in Hawaii. The catch was that I had to raise $5,000 for the Diabetes Association. It was a fundraiser thing and then I go and run a marathon. I made the commitment and had been training daily. I was up to running about fifteen miles with a seven-minute mile. Raising the money was the hard part. I sent out letters for support and picked up about seven to eight hundred dollars in cash, far away from my goal. I didn't know what to do to get this money. I had thought of everything and time was running out. I felt pretty comfortable that something would pop up and everything would work out fine. I had some pretty cool people in my life that enjoyed helping me out, but when it came down to it, it was me that put it all together.

I decided to produce a commercial and have the client pay to be mentioned for supporting the Diabetes Association. This ended up bringing in the money I needed to run the marathon.

Chapter Sixteen

I remember Mandy telling me that I would meet my soul mate while working at the health store. She felt that this was a place where the right-minded guy would appear. While working there, a few guys did appear, but they were all either married or just too weird for me. Really at this point in my life, I was quite comfortable being without a man. I still liked to date, but I was just not interested in forcing something to work just because I had a void to fill. The men came and went. Then one day while working I got a phone call. Actually, the guy left a message and after listening to his voice I thought I would call him back. I was studying up on a product called HGH at the time and the message was asking for information on HGH. I was also very into signs. It was a sign that he called just at the right moment when I was reading about HGH, I would be a fool to not call him back. Right away I loved his voice and wanted to see him in person, so I invited him into the store to talk in more detail about this product. This was all in my head of course; he didn't think anything about it except to get the information he wanted. I took this job pretty seriously since I was really into health and fitness. I wanted to know what every pill would or wouldn't do. HGH (if your not familiar) is a human

193

growth hormone. So, this guy comes in to talk with me about this product. I can remember quite clearly. He came in and my first impression was holy shit! He was beautiful! He had incredibly big muscles. His arms were the size of my thighs, and his face… oh so chiseled! He was so handsome and aware. I liked this guy from the moment I saw him! Yes, it was physical at first but we talked and the more we did that I found out we were on the same spiritual path. We were reading the same material and he was a Reiki master. He was actually taking classes at the same place that I was! He also worked out at the same gym that I did! This was too perfect in my mind until… "Hi, can I help you." "Oh, Schelli, this is my wife." All of my energy came crashing to the floor! He was fucking married and she was about the most ugly bitch I had ever seen. My mind could not wrap around this information. She had this neurotic energy. He was so soft, kind and gentle and gorgeous! She was out of shape; short, boyish looking and it just didn't work for me! I never let on to anything that I was thinking of course. I just played it as business and treated her no different. By the end of the conversation I found out that the wife didn't like to work, but worked in video and he was trying to push her into working for me. I didn't resist this; I could always use another shooter, but her…why not? I let it go, and decided to not judge. I gave her a shout, but it was up to her to make the call. They left and it was a while later before the phone rang.

Ester ended up calling me after Mike had pushed her into it. Mike, that was is his name, and his wife, Ester. Mike had spent the past thirty years of his life driving trucks and Ester just spent his money. She wasn't one to work. That was obvious once I decided to let her work for me. Half of the time she was sick or late but the bottom line was that she just wasn't good at it. I had set up a meeting with the Red Cross to do a production for them. I thought this would be a good opportunity for Ester to go along and learn how to sell a long form production. She and I were spending quite a bit of time together; not just business, but personal as well. Again with all of my so-called knowledge I thought I was helping her understand who she was. To understand that she created her reality and she had no one to blame but herself. I would try to talk with her about her illness but none of that ever sunk in. She was attached to her pain and wasn't going to give it up. I was growing tired of the whole "wedding business". I was thinking about having Ester run the company while I pursued other things. Having her go to the meeting was essential since selling is key in running your own business. I was always pretty good at it; I was just myself. Selling something that I really believed in was easy. Anyway back to the meeting. Ester ended up showing up late and making us late for the meeting. I didn't get upset about it; I was going with the flow and wanted to see how it would turn out. I apologized for being late and carried on with the meeting. After, Ester mentioned that it went well. I turned to her and said, "No, they will not book with us, being late was the end of it." She didn't agree, but it turned out that I was right! I have always been very good about being on time, always, and I just knew that we wouldn't get the gig because we were late!

I knew Ester was not the right choice for my company, but I was really getting tired of the whole thing and I was looking for a way out. I would still own my business; I would just let her run it. I was really confused. One day I liked her, the next I couldn't stand to be around her! I felt this way about Steve to. He was really getting on my nerves. He was never on time… and the drama!

I decided to go on a camping trip for a few days and asked Steve to watch Schekki. He stayed at my place, worked and watched the cat. I needed some time away. When I came home I felt so off, like something was wrong. I walked through the house and found the hot tub cover removed. I can't remember how this all came down to me, but it did! I found out that Steve had pretty much drank all the booze in my house, got in the hot tub, and then he decided to roam the neighborhood naked. The cops were called; Steve was arrested and barely got out of jail in time to shoot a wedding. Ester was on the job with Steve and was freaking out when he didn't show up. He did, but late. After talking with the neighbors I found out that another night when I was gone, early in the morning he had lifted all the blinds and stood naked in the window. I noticed once when I came home that my massage oils were next to the computer. You can figure that one out on your own. I had my moments with Steve and just didn't know how to handle it. He was stealing money from me. I was loaning him money as well, more like giving him money. I found out his car was going to get repossessed and I tried to help with that. They ended up taking the car anyway.

I left for New York to get ordained. Before I left I decided it was time to let Steve go. There was nothing I could do. I was so confused. I couldn't help him no matter how hard I tried and things were just getting worse. The business was falling flat and I needed to pull it back together again. I wanted to get ordained because I was sick and tired of the traditional weddings, tired of the Catholic crap. I wanted to offer a more personal ceremony if anyone was interested. I found this guy that does ordinations and headed off for New York. I was feeling terrible after letting Steve go and did much soul searching. Ester was as much of a pain in the ass as Steve and she bitched about him all the time. I also wanted to get rid of Ester. I wanted to just get rid of everyone and everything negative! The night before the ordination I got totally fucked up in the hotel bar. I was so hung over the next day but managed to make the ordination and drove home that night. In the drive home I decided to bring Steve back, that I was judging him and that I needed to accept him for who and what he was. I did just that and things were back to the way they were, or so it appeared for a very short moment.

My big marathon was approaching soon and I decided to have Ester watch over things while I was gone. The hot tub company was one company that sponsored me and also offered me a really good job selling for them. Once I left for Hawaii I knew I would be done working at the health store and was deciding on taking the job with the hot tub company to make some good money. I left to Hawaii for ten days all by myself; first to run a marathon and second to travel alone to the different Islands and spend some time trying to figure things out. The trip was amazing. I met this great person the first night. She and I became quick friends. I ran the 26.2 miles in five hours and nineteen minutes. I was completely drained but it was an incredible experience. I'm not sure at what mile I started hallucinating. After the marathon I did some Island hopping and just enjoyed myself. I really loved the Islands and knew I would return again.

Once all of that was over and things settled down a bit I decided to take the job at the hot tub company. This was a really tough thing to do; it interrupted my way of living. I was getting up at 5am, going for a run and then hitting the gym for a good hour to come home and start my day with the business. Business was really slow and I needed a better paying job. I was way over my head in debt and the ship was slowly sinking. So I took the job at the hot tub company and let Ester handle things at my video company with Steve doing the editing. I wasn't at the job for one week and I got really sick. I hated it, hated being told what time to be there and how to sell. I hated the whole corporate thing. Being told how to dress, how to act! I would find any reason possible to get out for a few hours instead of staring at an empty desk with a phone that never rang. One day I went home for lunch to find Steve and Ester stoned! That was it! I quit the job, took back my company and not too soon after Ester was history.

One night during my relationship with Ester, she and I went out and she introduced me to this guy that was a friend of hers. He and I hooked up a few times, but he became very needy and clingy. He actually brought his bikes and his boat over to my house so he could swing by anytime he wanted. I told him to get them out of my house and tried endlessly to finish the relationship. It took a while but he finally went away. He was so obnoxious; I grew tired of it! Most of the time I spent was for going within; I was on my journey and wanted to find out who I was. I started getting up even earlier to meditate. I would get up, drink a glass of lemon water and go into my trance. I'm not sure what that ever did for me, except I did manifest an incredible tattoo! Oh yeah, I was the all-knowing guru in my own mind.

I mentioned earlier that I was doing massage therapy and that was going really good. I had built a clientele and was really into it! Mike and I saw each other once in a while when I had a party and Ester dragged him along. He was never really into any of it, but he showed up and he and I always had great conversations. Mike also decided to let me massage him! The first time, I was scared to death, not to mention his wife was upstairs. I was terrified mainly because of his size. After one hour on a normal size dude I was tired, but Mike is no ordinary sized guy and I just wasn't sure what to do with him. I remember when he got on the table and his back was so huge it was sticking way up in the air. I took a deep breath and went for it. The first time was casual, yet it was good enough that he scheduled for his second massage with me.

Ester and I were hanging out one night when we got into a discussion about being cheated on. As you know Andy (my first and only marriage at this point) had cheated on me within the first few months of our marriage. I knew that no matter what, I would never let it go and even if we did stay together I would never let him live it down. I knew that even though it was hard to do, I had to let it go and end the relationship. Well, Ester was telling me that Mike had cheated on her and she would never let it go. She kept him in the marriage as a debt he owed to her. She had him so fooled it was crazy to me. She didn't trust him yet planted so much bullshit in his head that he would stay and try to make it up to her. I just couldn't believe she would want to live that way. She couldn't let him go though, since he paid her way and there was no other man that would ever want anything to do with her. So it was the guilt that kept him in the marriage. I just didn't get it and I still don't. What I feel about cheating is this: if you don't want to be there then it's time to go. It's that simple; don't drag it out and force it to work. If you are looking outside for something then you really just need to move on. We don't owe anyone on this planet anything. Love is fleeting when it's not love and most relationships, if not all, are superficial to begin with; most people just don't see it. I can't imagine trying to work it out when there is nothing to work out. It is what it is and you have to be aware enough to understand. This is your life, live it, stop being the victim. It took me a long time to get that. I did know that no counseling would mend what had happened and I didn't want it to. There is no way anyone should have to deal with that. Life does move on and it is only a memory and soon it's not even that. Ester went on and on about how she had Mike trapped and that he owed her big time. That she would never let that go. I felt sorry for her, but I also felt that I needed to share this with Mike. For whatever the reason, I just didn't give a shit that he cheated on her and all I could think about was how that was his first clue to get out of the marriage. But it didn't happen that way; he stayed for another twenty years- Oi Vei!

I really loved Mike in an unconditional way. He was very kind and gentle and he was very loyal to his marriage. I guess he figured since he was in it he may as well get through it. Later I found out how he really felt. For years he knew he couldn't leave because she would take him for everything and he just couldn't do it. He drove trucks and was gone most of the time anyway visualizing a new life for himself; a visualization that he manifested.

I just couldn't get over the hold that Ester had on Mike and after much contemplation I decided to have a chat with him before the massage we had scheduled. Mike and I sat down and had a nice long talk about what Ester had shared with me. He was so upset he started crying. He had no idea that she was still holding on to all of that and also that she was telling everyone. Twenty years later and still carrying this. This was the first time during massage that the energy was so intense! We had a connection that I still can't put into words and after that session I had no idea how my world and his were about to change.

Chapter Seventeen

A good friend that I had met while working at the health store introduced me to this guy that does past life regressions. My friend was totally sold on him and since he figured I had some men issues to work out he suggested I make an appointment. I did have men issues on many levels and I didn't see the harm in going. First, I was really into staying present. I was reading a Course In Miracles and started getting pretty hooked on energy and manifestation. Nothing is how it appears, there is no such thing as a mass, and everything is always moving in patterns. I was having some weird shit going on with March 10th and I got really obsessed by it. For some reason the men popping into my life were all born in March, I started to turn down anyone or anything that was March related. Ken was a March baby, Andy a March baby; Bart was born March 10th or so my memory serves me! I was sure that March was taboo and I just wasn't seeing the pattern! Then I found out Mike was a March baby! I thought going to see this guy would help me to understand why I was drawn in by the type of people I was. This included women as well, not just men; and not just relationships but my own destruction, my job choices. Why was I so ready to pick up and run all the time? I wanted answers but had yet to find anyone to give them to me: all of the spiritual books, the classes, and the reiki; on and on, and still no answers!

When I first got to the guy's house, I liked him right away. He was very likable and friendly. I sat in a chair across from him and he began his description of my past life. I have a tape of it today, but I honestly don't want to go back and listen to it, since I feel it is really nothing! And I mean nothing; it means nothing whether I was to believe in it or not. I will just go from memory to tell you what was said. I will also tell you that at this time I did believe it or more like I wanted to believe it! He told me many things that were hard to grasp. One is that I have been a man in most of my lives and I didn't want to come back and be a woman but I knew I had to in order to work out some of my karma. I guess I wasn't a very good man most of the time and that is why I draw mean and selfish men to me in this lifetime. I had something to do with Lincoln; I didn't understand, except that it had something to do with money and why I am the way I am with money. I was also a descendent of Jesus; I guess I carried this sword or something. On and on it went. I also am sun energy and Mike and I had an agreement when we were of the sun that we would meet again at some point in our different lives. Before I left he gave me

205

some exercises to help clear up my man issues; and yes, I did them. One exercise was to write a bunch of names on little pieces of paper and then burn them; this was a cleansing. Another was to meditate, and in meditation I was to visualize being in a theater. I would invite one man at a time to sit by me and there I would say that they are my mirror, that they are me and I take responsibility and let it go. I was really into it and I really felt the healing. Who knows really? I was so into it that I told Mike about it and he went right away to see this guy.

Mike also walked out blown away. This guy told him he was almost at Christ consciousness and would not come back again. He was in Dharma. He was a priest in the Horace Temple at one point; these were many powerful images for Mike. He was so into it that he came to see me right away! We talked about it and shared our tapes with each other. Mike went home and told Ester. Ester called and wanted to talk with me. I knew things had changed for Mike and I after the massage. We had a closer connection but then I remembered we had a connection to begin with, we just didn't do anything with it except have great talks when we saw each other! I will come back to the life regression part but first I want to share a time when a bunch of friends were all sitting in the kitchen. I had quite a few people over for drinks and a BBQ and Mike was in the kitchen, cleaning; yeah, cleaning. I really enjoyed being around him so I sat there and he and I talked. He started to tell me about his brother that just recently died from alcohol. Mike I guess hadn't had a drink in eighteen years until he started hanging out with my group. He still didn't drink much just one cocktail or two. His brother died from alcohol and I would say this is when Mike started seeking more than what he had been told most of his life. He often told me that he felt his brother was way deep into the rabbit's hole and no one could get him. He grew tired, tired of this life and wanted out! I learned a lot about how Mike felt about things. He had gone through some interesting things. At the same time his brother was dying his mother was in the hospital, dying as well. My talks with Mike were deep, not shallow "how is the weather?" bullshit. We really got into the exploring of things and I really enjoyed it. I didn't have many people that I could "go deep" with. Most were so caught up in their own beliefs that they couldn't get past that door; shit, they didn't even want to knock on the door to see who would answer. I was always irritated when trying to talk with someone who held tight to his or her beliefs and wouldn't even consider looking at it in another way. Ester was one of them. When she called and wanted to come over and talk about how Mike "was changing," I didn't even want to bother with her, but I knew I had to make an effort. Mike went back on the road for a couple of days and we kept in touch on the phone.

Ester and I were sitting at the bar in my condo and she was going on and on about how "she is losing him", "he thinks he is better than her," this, that and a bunch of shit. I just couldn't walk her through. For as long as she and I hung out we had always talked about her and Mike's relationship or how she thought it was. I remember one day driving down the road and her saying, "Don't you wish you could have what I have?" I just about lost it laughing! Hell no, I don't want a guy that I am forcing to be with me. I don't want a superficial relationship; I have had plenty of those! She just didn't understand why I would choose to be alone over just settling for anyone. Of course, she couldn't, and I wasn't about to explain otherwise. I just laughed. On many occasions I had just felt so sorry for Mike. I could see through it all but kept my distance on ever saying anything. It was his life; he chose it he would have to figure it out. By this time I had learned that it didn't matter what I said anyway, people did what they did and no amount of my insight will change anything.

Mike had been driving truck for a really long time; he ended up buying his own truck and was on the road most of the time. He made a lot of money that he didn't see much of. All he did was work and by now he was growing really tired. He tried on many occasions to talk with Ester about getting out of the business. They owned some (more like Mike owned) property and he knew he could sell it off to pay off the truck and find a way to get out of the trucking business. Ester would hear nothing of it! I sat right there one night and tried to help him find a way out of the business and Ester was livid that I would suggest such a thing. She was terrified of her secure, little world being shattered! I just turned to Mike and said, "If you want it bad enough, you will have to make it happen!" I knew that he would. I had no doubts; this guy was so talented in so many ways I just couldn't see him driving a truck until his death!

So here Ester was pouring out all of her selfish shit on me and I just wanted to shove it back in her face! I didn't, I just listened and asked her what life would be like for her without Mike in it! She cried and cried; I guess that was a hard question! Attachment! It was for her good of course. I can remember how it used to feel when I was so attached that I couldn't stand to let that person go. I would ache all over. But my point was "life

209

with out attachment" and again, it was going nowhere. I knew things were coming to a close with the relationship. Things happened so fast; I never had time to second-guess anything. I personally wanted to get rid of Ester a long time back, but my feeling sorry for her stopped me! I hate that part. She puts on this look of "nobody likes me and my life sucks; I just need a friend" and I become the sucker! But I knew it would eventually happen, doing something I didn't want to didn't last too long; eventually I would end it altogether.

I also knew something was going to happen with Mike, I could feel it. Yet I didn't have a clue to what. He had told me that he had been done with the marriage for a really long time. Mike and I are friends; we talk, we share, not to gain each other's approval or to get me to sleep with him. It was not like that ever. He was not like that. I on the other hand really wanted to have sex with him! That just wasn't what our friendship was about. He shared many things with me that he had never even spoken about. I knew he was leaving Ester, I just didn't know when or where he would go. I was just an ear for him.

That night, after Ester left I was pretty wound up. I was feeling all of this rising up and not knowing what to do. Mike called. We talked for a long time. His truck broke down and he was having it towed back, then he planned to head over to the house and tell Ester he was leaving. He had made up his mind; he was done. I asked him where he was going to go and he said, "I don't know, but I know where I would like to go." I was speechless. I hadn't thought of this, I knew I loved this man I just didn't think he was thinking that way. I knew I would never pursue it. When he said that, I realized he did want to be with me. I had been living in this condo without a man for two years, was I ready for this? My head was swimming and I knew in my heart how I felt. I knew I couldn't carry the past around with me. I knew also that I had waited my whole life for this kind of a relationship -- unconditional. I knew it existed, I just didn't find it until I found Mike. I didn't want to think, I just wanted to go with it and not allow my ego to get into the conversation. I agreed that he could come stay with me and that was that. We hung up and as I walked away I said out loud "I love you, Mike." The phone rang and it was Mike calling back. He said, "I love you too." I just about lost it; my legs were so wiggly I could barley walk down the stairs. I didn't sleep a wink that night knowing that he was coming to live with me the next day. Holy shit, I haven't even kissed the man. I hope he's a good kisser; a bad kisser can ruin everything! It was October 31st, Halloween, when Mike showed up. In the back of my mind I had my reservations. I had been involved with married men before and they never did what they said they were going to do. Then again I knew that I had slept with all of them and they just said what they said for whatever reason. I had to believe that this was true, but I also told myself if he chickens out and doesn't leave her that is fine as well. He is first my friend and I am not attached to the outcome. It was his life and he had to live it without any interference from me. Needless to say I was totally excited when the knock came at the door and YES, I opened it. Opened it to the unknown, opened it to the possibilities, opened it for Love. He walked in, our eyes met and we shared our first kiss! The shoe fits!

Chapter Eighteen

The next couple of weeks were a whirlwind! When Ester found out that Mike was coming to stay with me (Mike told her) she immediately assumed we had been having an affair for a long time! I knew she was coming over and I was ready for her. Before I get into the female bashing section I first want to express to my readers how I feel now about relationships/ownership! Nobody owns anyone, period! If you are having issues; if you want out, get out! Forget counseling. Why try to repair something that in truth is not broken? You are just changing and changing without that person. Forget the guilt trip. You have the right to live however you want to live. If people don't like it, too bad! It's not personal nor will it ever be. Respect that the person wants to move on and let them. You can't force a relationship to work and why would you want to? I think we get way to weird about relationships and marriage. Does anyone even know where and how marriage began? I feel that you can walk whenever you want in marriage or not. It blows my mind that just because someone said "I do" thirty years ago that they feel indebted to stay in a nightmare relationship. I can go on and on about this, but how I feel is that there are no exceptions to unconditional love, none! When you condition the relationship you are bound to live in chaos! And live you will; out of fear you will never leave and out of fear you will play a game that is not worth playing. I know for sure that unconditional love does exist and I will never settle for anything less! Kids or no kids, stop living your lie and wake the fuck up!

I hope I wasn't too rough, but it is a passionate subject for me! So, Ester comes over with her big badass sister. Mike was downstairs sleeping since he was on the road for a few days and was extremely tired. I went outside to talk with Ester but she didn't say much of anything. It was her sister that went off on me, telling me that she knows girls like me, stealing other women's husbands; a slut basically is what she was calling me. Ester was positive that Mike and I had been having an affair and there was nothing I could say to convince her otherwise. She was so upset that she brushed passed me and ran into the house, ran downstairs to Mike sleeping in the bed and pulled the covers off him to find him naked. That was it, she was now sure that we were having sex. I went back in the house and stood in the kitchen. Ester came up then a few minutes later Mike came up and went outside to talk with the two. Finally this came to an end and they left. Mike went back to bed. Many long days and nights came with all of the drama that Ester was creating. She just would not accept the fact that Mike and I were not having sex. I got a call a few days later from my mom. She told me some woman had called and talked to Dad. She said I had been sleeping with her husband and I took him away from her. She wanted my dad to do something about it. He basically told her I was a grown woman and I would do whatever I wanted and hung up. I laughed my ass off when my mom told me this, I couldn't believe she would call my parents! Her plan was to try to go to my family where they would not like Mike. It didn't work of course. I had a nice talk with my parents and once they met Mike they really liked him.

Mike and I really got into some heavy shit with energy and thought. We were going deep and pretty much locked ourselves inside to go inside. I remember the first time my parents met Mike. I had just finished up a massage when my mom knocked on the door. My parents would always just show up at my place without notice. This time my dad stayed in the car and Mom came to the door, I took Mike and we went outside to meet my dad. My dad was really weird about coming in; I think he was really uncomfortable with the way I lived but that didn't stop him from coming up un-announced. Remember, Mike is a big guy, and the look on my dads face was of shock! I think he was just blown away by his size, but once they met, he couldn't help but love Mike; Mike is just too kind and gentle.

Things didn't clear up for a really long time. Mike's kids were extremely upset and he had to deal with all of that the best he could. I really didn't get hung up in all of that. I knew I was living my life for me and I didn't give a shit about anyone else. Mike's dad really liked me and so did his stepmom. They came by to visit and we had some really nice conversations. We were now approaching the holidays. Mike and I still did the holiday thing at this point but we questioned it and decided to do it for family and to leave our feelings out of it. Mike's dad invited us over for Thanksgiving and this is where I got to face the kids. I really didn't want to go, but I knew I had to keep myself grounded and be okay with whatever was to happen. The kids treated me like shit but I didn't mind. I knew that they were going to feel however they were going to feel and until they understood the whole story that wouldn't change. I am, after all, the other woman that destroyed a twenty-something year marriage. Ester had pretty much told everyone that I was sleeping with her husband; that I befriended her just to steal her man. She had gone into the gym that I worked out at and told some people in there whom I had actually became friends with the story and from then on everyone in there treated me like shit too. They could barely make eye contact with me. I was simply amazed at what was going on. People believed her story without even talking to me, and the funny thing is that Mike and I were still not having sex. We were getting to know each other and that was the best part.

Mike didn't waste any time with getting the divorce underway. He had to go back to his house to pick up a few things. Ester would corner him and try to get him to come back to her. That didn't work, he had his mind made up, and he was done. Mike has three kids, two are from his first marriage and one is with Ester. All three kids are grown and out of the house, yet they still felt compelled to butt in to Mike's choices. They all felt once you were married you stayed married, they felt that way when it came to their parents, but not so much in their own lives. It was a blow to what they thought a relationship was. He wasn't allowed to change. He did though and without their consent. Ester decided she wasn't going to let him serve her, so she got an attorney and sued him for the divorce first. I remember when he got the papers and we had to sit with it. Mike owned the house they were living in; he owned the property next to the house as well. He owned his own trucking company and was the one that paid the bills and all of her medical crap. He basically did everything and here she was trying to get it all. It was no surprise to me, but I did feel that Mike should get an attorney and try to negotiate it out. She was really unbelievable with all her wants. She bought from me this exercise machine called the Total Gym to give to Mike; that was in the divorce papers for something she wanted. There were the little petty things, and of course all of the big things. Mike got this attorney, who was a complete joke. She pretty much said that Ester would get whatever she wanted and Mike should be happy to not have to pay alimony. I was willing to fight, but Mike was tired and he had no attachments to the material. It was a long haul or so it felt like, but it did come to a close and he did give it all away. The house was sold and she got the money; the land was sold and she got the money. He was fine with it; he just wanted out and didn't feel like fighting.

During all of this Mike and I became extremely close. We talked about everything, explored everything and one night while we were out watching my friend's band we met this guy Eric that introduced us to Kristnamurti's *Freedom From the Known* and from that read on, our lives shifted dramatically. Mike and I use to meditate together every morning,

218

and if he was on the road we would meditate together through distance. We manifested our first tattoo together through meditation and we both had that stamped on our lower backs. We also started a kitty cause we wanted to go to Tibet. We had so many incredible experiences together; it was wonderful to be sharing this existence with someone like Mike. I was so happy and so very much in love for the first time in my life!

The drama did continue but Mike and I had removed ourselves from much of it. We decided to not get involved and that eventually the truth would come out, but we really felt that it was nobody's business how and why we got together. We were going to live our lives together. Most of my life has revolved around sex and for the first time in my life I was in a relationship that had nothing to do with sex. Once we decided to be intimate it was incredible. I never had a man that pleased me first, that took the time for lovemaking. The orgasms were endless. The sex was a bonus, but it had nothing at all to do with our relationship. We were growing spiritually and that meant more to me than any of it. We were open to everything! One day he and I were out and this old man came up to us and kept saying, "take me home, take me home." We couldn't figure him out, he barely spoke English and we didn't know how to help him.

219

We put him in the car and drove by his direction and ended up at this house. It turns out he wandered from home and didn't know how to get back. We took a chance and took him home. The people were gracious. We were living by signs; if it showed up we were open to seeing where it took us.

Winter was on and Mike and I were getting restless. We decided it was time for a road trip. We packed our bags and headed west not sure where we would end up. We really just wanted to have some fun and follow the pyramid. We kept seeing the pyramid everywhere and really felt like it was a sign. Silly stuff, but we were pretty much into it. We were hooked on Krisnamurti and were reading all of his books together. Our trip ended in Sedona, Arizona. Once we drove down the canyon and took in the fresh air and the beautiful red rock views we knew we were hooked. Our first day there we went to a rental place, found a house and waited to see if we could get in. Mike and I were pacing, trying to figure out the money part and if we should go for it. I recall walking down a road called Inspiration Drive where we talked about making the move. This lady came out and I noticed a sign in her window that said DJ? I asked her about the wedding business and found it was a very popular place for weddings. We went into this other place to get a feel for the market and here we met a photographer that gave us the name of a video producer that could help us out. Everything was just falling into place. It was so easy, so right and we didn't second-guess it. We got into the house that we are now renting and spent a week in contemplation.

December 25.

We are this one energy. Love only in silence while you know who you are. One energy exploded into a form to experience. Too many thousands of incarnations. Thousands more. Arizona 2003 Christmas -- not sure how to explain our discovery today. We have been alone together, empty house, silence -- meditation -- the energy is amazing here and we are just being, experiencing more about who we are. Mike and I are moving, we are going for it and in all this we are learning, healing and growing. It amazes me how incredible I feel -- I just live to be this changing flowing energy of life and to not get caught in the tick tock drama. I am so at peace with him and if I can share, it would be to not waste away with what everyone else thinks about. Find your call and live -- you and I are no different -- I just won't live a life that isn't for my highest purpose. I will no longer be drawn into the lives of others that choose to be victims. I am responsible for all that I am right now. I won't be controlled by money and I will be me. Love -- life -- eternity and I will spend the rest of my days living. Life and love are one. I know when I look at Mike I see and feel the essence of who I am, the only separation is the body and the conditioning -- when you can see past that you will be still and know that I am God -- through these life experiences I heal in this human form -- I touch -- I taste -- I smell -- and in every human relationship I learn more about who I am. This is truly only a blink. So why, why spend your days with worry and anger and hate? Let things be as they may, for when you resist you're truly living in an anguished illusion. Love, Love is everything!

Mike made a few phone calls about selling his truck; I called Donna about selling the condo and it all just fell into place. Mike sold the truck, the condo went up for sale and a month later it was sold. We headed back to Michigan to get things in order. We were so excited we drove straight through and never stopped.

Chapter Nineteen

Everything was really going great. We sold all of the big stuff that we didn't want and closed all of our affairs in Michigan. We bought a trailer and filled it; it took two trips from Michigan to Sedona to move everything, but that was fine since we had business to settle in Michigan anyway. The final day, I officiated my first wedding. We finished packing and left Michigan for good; on to new and wonderful opportunities.

Mike's kids were not happy at all about the move; they felt like they were being abandoned. Brent, his youngest had decided to get married and also decided that I wasn't invited. Money was really tight. Somehow we managed to make it work. To this day I have no idea how we did it, but we did! Once we got settled into Sedona, I started making the calls to get work. Sedona is a different world than what I was used to. In Michigan I was doing big high-end weddings and a lot of television commercials. Sedona is a destinations place and we had to join this association just to get noticed; not to mention all of the weddings were small and planners were a huge part of the business. I had never worked with planners in Michigan; I booked my own gigs. Not in Sedona though, I had to think differently about the business. After some adjustments and some meet and greets the business started to come and it wasn't too long before we were doing really great! I sold my Jeep and we went down to just one vehicle. We sold a lot of stuff just to keep our bills paid. When I look back on it now, it seems as though it all worked out with no stress, yet I'm sure I was freaking out a few times wondering how we were going to pull it off.

The first year in Sedona we went back to Michigan all summer to finish up wedding work; we had over seventeen gigs to finish. This was very tough! Oh, before I forget, Brent did get married and Mike never went. He decided he didn't want to deal with the Ester drama nor did he have any interest in the "marriage game". Brent was really pissed and wouldn't speak to Mike for a long time. Mike figured he would work it out for himself as he did eventually. So here we are, traveling back and forth to Michigan. We stayed at Mike's dad's house when we were there. We had all of our equipment in his basement so when we couldn't get back we just had Steve do the shoot then send us the footage to edit. Mike and I also hired this other couple to do some shooting. This was a really bad idea; the footage was coming back to us all dark and barely visible. It was a nightmare editing this crap footage and I got so pissed off that I decided to not pay this couple and fire them! It was crazy but we managed to wrap it up and be done with Michigan.

While we were doing the drive we would read to each other from Krishnamurti. During one of the trips we got hit with the biggest realization! Nothing, we are nothing! We are nothing more than memories, thoughts, our programming and conditioning; in truth we are nothing! What I remember is this hitting me so hard I had to pull over. It was a strange feeling to feel that! Mike and I didn't get much of a chance to bond with Sedona the first year, since we spent most of it in Michigan. We got so tired of doing the drive that we decided to fly back. Mike and I were also doing some heavy inquiry on death and intuitiveness. This trip would be one we wouldn't soon forget. I remember having dinner with Mike's dad and Norma. We made our yummy salmon and asparagus dish. We were just sitting around the table talking when Norma started choking. We all stopped to make sure she was ok and then carried on. That night we were heading out to meet my friends Shawn and Mel for a couple of drinks. I am not a big one for sitting down at the table for dinner with family anymore since everyone feels so inclined to pray; I have at this point in my life stopped the whole praying business. I used to feel obligated to do so and eventually decided to just not participate in it and let them do what they felt they had to do. Mike's dad was pretty cool about all of it and he stopped doing the whole prayer thing to. My parents are a different story. Anyway, I know I wander; I guess that gives you a good feel on how my mind operates. So we finished up with dinner and headed off. It was nice seeing Mel and Shawn again; we got into this big talk on death. When Mike and I left the house we were talking about how the house felt like death. I just couldn't put my finger on it, but we agreed that it felt like they or one of them was just waiting around to die. It was an eerie feeling, but one that we had to talk about. I have always been intrigued with death. I have no problem talking about it, but most people like to avoid it like the plague! Shawn didn't buy into any of what we were trying to say at the table. It was like talking to a wall and I was just getting more and more aggravated. Mike always keeps his cool. He just speaks about how he looks at it and then lets it go. I on the other hand can't let it go! Why is death so taboo? What are we afraid of? We have been taught our whole lives that death is not good; heaven and hell, being saved, being burned…and the truth is we have no idea what happens when the body dies. People sure like to think they do though. I really have no idea, but it's a fun topic and I love talking about it. Most people fear it for themselves, not for other people. When they lose someone they love it is just self-serving but still it is a loss and that person is then faced with their own demise. Interesting subject! Mel and Shawn thought we were pretty rude for talking about the feeling of death in the house but our point was more about what we were feeling and to just have the awareness. We went on and on and finally the night came to a close. I was getting pretty fucked up so we decided to go. Once I get to this state, I am pretty much useless; I drift off into my own dark world. I talked Mike into going to another bar so I could get even more drunk, anything to avoid what I was feeling. Down the dark drama hole I went, dragging poor Mike with me. Mike and I like to enjoy a drink or two but he had yet to experience me crossing over and honestly I didn't want him to ever have to go through that, but he did and this wouldn't be the last time.

I can never remember what happens so I have to rely on what Mike tells me. I went into the "feel sorry for Schelli" stage and left the bar, went out to find a tree and sat under it. I told Mike to leave me there, that I would find someone else to take care of me. He of course didn't leave. I cried and talked a bunch of nonsense until he finally did something to get me to go home. Once we got back to his dad's I remember Norma insisting I take some B6 to help with my hangover in the morning. That was the last time I saw her alive. Mike was woken by his Dad at around 2am. He came downstairs and said, "I need your help, Norma is not breathing." Mike ran upstairs to find Norma lying on her back, obviously dead. Mike looked at his dad who stood in shock, and knew that he had to at least attempt revival with CPR. Mike proceeded to do mouth to mouth and had instructed his dad to call 911. The E-unit arrived, the two attendants continued to administer CPR, but it was too late. There was no bringing her back. The next thing I hear is Mike saying, "Schelli, Schelli, get up, Norma is dead!" Man, I sprung to my feet, still drunk, trying to grasp what Mike just said to me! It was so surreal.

Mike and I talked endlessly about that night, trying to understand the signs. Why had I gotten so drunk? All the talk in the world didn't seem to make a difference; what is, is!

The funeral was another thing. I was really uncomfortable being in the house with all of Mike's family around. I just didn't feel like it was my place and I honestly wanted to just run from it! I hated to leave Mike but I felt it was the thing to do, so I took off to Mandy's for a night to clear my head. I liked Norma; she was a nice lady. My thoughts on death had changed and I couldn't explain that. One night away and I really missed Mike, so I headed back and decided to go to the funeral with him. The night before, they had the "showing". I didn't go to that. This gave Ester the opportunity to try one more time to get Mike back. Funny, how we use death as a way to benefit ourselves. I guess she missed him but didn't leave without making sure to pass off some old wedding photos. Pretty sad, huh? She didn't come to the funeral, that in itself was a challenge. I decided to go and be available for Mike and Diane, Norma's daughter, Mike's brother's wife. You can figure that out for yourself. Sitting there listening to some man that thinks he has a direct link to God talking about Norma being in heaven was a bit much for Mike and I. Like this guy knew all of the secrets and the rest of us were just stupid asses believing everything he says. Puke! My heart went out for Mike's dad the most. He is such a sweet guy, and has endured a few deaths: his first wife, Mike's mom and his son. Mike's mom died from ALS, Lou Gehrig's disease, and he had to take care of her for a really long time. Mike's brother died from alcohol disease; Mike's dad cared for him, also. Now Norma, out of the blue, was dead!

We were picked up from the airport by Norma and Dad, and dropped off at the airport without Norma. It was weird. We got back to Sedona and it was a long time before we went back to Michigan. Mike's Dad has come out often to visit, which has been really cool. My parents have yet to make the trip and I suspect they never will.

April 10, 2004

Easter Sunday -- a day created by religion -- I haven't written in so long. I grabbed to actually write my dream. I know what dreams consist of. I'm not so quick to want to record them. Yet it is the minds continued continuity. I dreamed Tom had died. Lynn and Tom and I were trying to talk about death with Lynn. She cried and cried, I cried. I felt this feeling on how she was so attached to him and now he was truly gone. She couldn't handle it. I was waiting somewhere to collect some money and it wasn't as much as I thought. Tom was alive hiding in my truck wanting to run away. Yet, I knew he died. He really didn't die. Die to every moment, my lucid dreams will cease when I do this. Now, I am in Sedona Arizona, looking out these big windows, the wind chimes are going good. It is quite windy with big open blue skies. Schekki gets my attention, to be fed. He starts to climb up on a plant to get my attention, so funny to watch him. I have no desire for writing anymore. I sit here and try to think of something to say and thought is old, what is the point for expression? Outwardly? No, there is no reason for this anymore my search is over.

Chapter Twenty

One year at our first home in Sedona and the house went up for sale; the rent went up as well. We decided to move into a small condo and that is where we stayed for four years. The first house is where we came to realize that Sedona was no different than Michigan, just a different religion/dogma. The spiritual marketplace is no different than the organized religions; they are still rooted in belief. Mike and I eventually gave up on meditating and all of that nonsense and started living. Mike and I would get up in the morning and share our dreams. I dreamed that Melissa was pregnant; I should share with you that her and Shawn had been trying to get pregnant for a very long time and nothing was happening. They were on all sorts of fertility drugs and were spending a lot of money and still nothing was happening. Mike thought I should call them and share my dream with them; I did this and found out that it was the day before that they got word that Mel was pregnant. I do still have dreams that get me to follow up, but I ask, what does it matter, I mean really? Think about that. Once when I was running I had a very distinct feeling of a heart attack, not me, but someone. Mike talked to his brother and found out that he had just had a heart attack. Again, what does it mean; what can I do? Nothing. It is just something to be aware of I guess, but I still have no clue as to what to do with it. Mike and I are very much mind readers with one another. Some of the things that have happened with us are just too hard to verbalize and I still have to ask why does it matter? It is what it is.

He and I are still very active with working out and I still run as much as I can. My energy has dropped a lot since I moved to the desert but I keep on keeping on, one way or another. There is really nothing to do in Sedona; we hike, we walk, we work, we read, we talk, we make love, we are happy, or are we? We are drinking almost everyday, myself more than Mike. I still need my escape, my drama. There are moments I don't feel worthy of this love, this life. I pull into the past and push Mike away. I will fall so many more times and he will just keep on loving me, and why? There is no answer to my questions, my fears, and my doubts. All of these years, all of this suffering and I have actually found myself in a relationship that will last as long as I am breathing and at times I still feel lost; afraid that he will give up on me and leave. All of these silly fears from memories; not really understanding that it's the fear, bottom line, fear that is killing me.

Sedona is a different world for weddings and commercial work. Most of the weddings are destination weddings. I would say ninety-nine percent are and that means less money. We don't do the big huge weddings we did in Michigan. Mike had talked about adding photography to bring in more money. I just didn't want to get into it. I felt video was competitive enough but photography was very competitive and backstabbing. We had no competition here in video; first, very few people do it and the ones that do are so bad it's an embarrassment to even be associated. In any given city you can have a few video people and a million photographers. Everyone wants to be a photographer! Since Mike and I are such a great team we often had people ask if we do both video and photos and more and more it was in our faces to just take on photography. We did and it was the best thing we could have done! We have stayed in Sedona and in business because of it!

We have produced many commercials and some music videos for a guy we met in Phoenix! I love doing the music videos; they are so much fun and a great creative release! I am still amazed to this day how people will opt for photos and not do video! Seriously folks, do I really need to explain this? It's life: moving, emotion, sound! Mike is really more the photographer; I still love doing the video. We have a great balance and the thing is that we can do both! It's all so fleeting really! Outside of work there really isn't much to do here. I bore easily and need some form of entertainment and if I don't get it I turn to the drink.

One night we were out partying with some friends and I got totally trashed. I put a wine glass under the car tire and called Mike all sorts of names. He left, ran over the glass, went down the road then turned around and came back. I was so drunk I had no idea he had even left. I ended up throwing up and getting extreme chest pains. Mike stayed; he cares for me. I wake up and he is there -- Unconditional. I take a Motrin, smoke a cigarette and I leave. I don't know where I went but I know how I came back. Mike was calling my name, telling me to come back. I left my body. Everything went black, everything was gone; my breathing became very shallow and he called for me and I came back. The death experience, my death experience! I'm not afraid of death. I am afraid of what death takes and that would be Mike! I love him so completely; I can't bear to give up my life with him. This is attachment. I know that, and I don't care! He is the one thing that keeps me here on the planet. Without him, I have no interest in being here anymore. He knows me, he knows the "me" that is not my past, not my conditioning. He feels the inner being and he loves me no matter what stupid things I do. We don't bother with petty things; we embrace what we have in the moment, knowing it could very well be our last.

Since we had been in Sedona, Mike's dad had been out three times. His oldest son came once, Mike's brother and wife once. My friend Gretchen came to visit once and my sister in law and niece came out once. Out of all the visits the one I dreaded the most was my sister in law. I don't have a relationship with these people and I was sick to my stomach thinking about it. I don't support the way these kids are being raised, and without going into it too much I have just one funny story to tell. We spent the whole day taking them around Sedona, up into the Red Rocks, down into the canyon. It was getting a bit chilly. We had the top of the Jeep down and Mike pulled over to give Kayla his jacket. Once we got to our spot, her and Felica went into the bathroom; we didn't notice it at first until later when we were looking at the photos. The coat that Mike gave Kayla to wear was inside out and later I came to figure it out. Mike didn't give her the coat inside out, they turned it inside out because it was Mikes coat and it was gross to wear it. Mike has tattoos and I can only imagine that she was told to turn it inside out so she didn't get Mike's cooties! I was showing her our video from our Florida trip and Felica had to cover Kayla's eyes for most of it! I tried to talk with Kayla but she is so conditioned from her parents she knows no different. She is totally hooked on the whole Jesus story and is blind to any other religious system. At lunch they go into their praying thing and I tried to tell her that people in Sedona don't pray, but they send energy to their food. It was like I couldn't say anything to that kid without Felica putting her beliefs on the child! What really disturbed me the most was that she was a 14-year-old girl. She had no emotions, no laughter in her life. She couldn't watch movies; Superman came on and she had never seen it! She didn't dance; she was joyless, just like her mother! Suppressed and it's sad! Why do parents push their beliefs on their children? Why can't the kids learn about it all and decide for themselves? Shutting them out, keeping them locked away; this really hits a nerve with me but at the same time I know there is nothing I can do, everything happens just as it will and I need not interfere. My parents did the same with me, I just didn't accept any of it as truth and found my own way. I can only hope these kids do the same! I asked Kayla if she would stay in Indiana or get out and travel and she said she would never leave her parents, she would stay close!

Just because we have families doesn't mean we have to go along with them. It took me forever to take my stand on that. And you know what? It's okay! When Mike and I went to visit my mom and dad, Dad would always bring up going to church. I flat out refused. I will never go to church again unless I am working a wedding and that is even pushing it! I won't pray at the table, but that doesn't mean they can't! I love my parents. My mom believes in the bible one hundred percent. She believes in God and that is fine if that is what she wants, but I don't! We are taught to just go along with it all and not question any of it... well I do question it and at one point was afraid to stand alone with it, but now I do and if people don't like it, that's fine; I just don't care! I am not going to live my life faking it anymore, just getting along! I'm done. I have Mike, he and I think alike. I have Mandy, we connect; not on everything, but we don't judge each other, we share. And I have Margaret, a friend here in Sedona who I connect with, and we tend to just laugh at all of it now! One big dream and one huge illusion that we take so seriously! I plan on doing whatever I want and laughing all the way through it! That also means no more visitors that make me sick!

Five years had passed since I had been back to Michigan. Since Mike and

I had been in Sedona we have gone to Hawaii twice, Vegas twice, Colorado, California three times, Seattle, Mexico, Florida and the Bahamas. I had no interest in going back to Michigan. I received a call from a bride in Michigan and decided this would be a good time to go back, we could work and also visit. Michigan has become so depressing; I could feel the shift happening as soon as we hit Missouri. So busy, so judging; I could barely stomach it. The first visit was to Mandy. Mandy and I had been staying in touch since the big move and I missed her. It was great seeing her but I soon understood that life goes on and it should. I had a life to live with Michael, her life was not mine; I will never make a difference in it and why should I try? I don't live the way she does. I took a different road: no kids, no marriage, no husband, no rules, and no limits! Mandy has been in Michigan her whole life. That is her life. She has been married forever and has four grown kids. Not my style; never was, never will be. I love her just the same! My oldest friend Lynn wouldn't even take the time to see me. We did end up meeting at a bar with her so-called boyfriend who I just as well could have gone the rest of my life never knowing. I was hurt she wouldn't leave the boyfriend for one night to come hang out with me. I was just so depressed in the visiting thing that I gave it up and just crashed that night. Mike and I went to his brother's and

I once again got totally fucked up. We snuck out in the morning and got a hotel. The rest of the trip was ok. I really just wanted to get it over with and we all know that is not the way to live! Of course I love Mike's Dad and that was all good; it was visiting Mike's kids, well only one really. His daughter has finally come to actually like me. His oldest son is kind but I can tell he doesn't really care for me. I know his wife doesn't; they are totally rooted in their Christian beliefs. The youngest was the one where I said "OK, I'm done with all of this, let's head to Traverse City." Five years later and Mike's son's wife asks me, "tell me the truth about what happened with Mike. Your story, not Mike's!" Five years later and she wants me to tell her a story that is different than Mikes? She wants me to justify myself to her... to her! I played her silly game, ate her food and really just wanted out!

I never wanted kids; I never wanted a relationship with a man that had kids. Mike's kids had grown up. I thought I was safe. My life is with Mike; I am not now nor have I ever been concerned with how his kids feel about me. I can't even imagine butting into my parents life; telling them who they can love or not, telling them that they can't get divorced if they want to! I can't imagine that. What is it that gives someone the right to ask

240

for someone else to sacrifice how he or she lives to make someone else

happy?

Conclusion

As quick as we left, we were back, a blink. Isn't that what this life is? A blink. I like Sedona. It offers the same drama that a big city does in a small way. I have become more of a recluse. The only drama I get anymore is the drama I create, and I do that on purpose for something to do. Soon that will pass too. I am just tired of the silly games people play and I choose to stay far away.

You should never be here too much; be so far away that they can't find you, they can't get at you to shape, to mould. Be so far away, like the mountains, like the unpolluted air; be so far away that you have no parents, no relations, no family, no country; be so far away that you don't know even where you are. Don't let them find you; don't come into contact with them too closely. Keep far away where even you can't find yourself; keep a distance, which can never be crossed over; keep a passage open always through which no one can come. Don't shut the door for there is no door, only an open, endless passage; if you shut any door, they will be very close to you, then you are lost. Keep far away where their breath can't reach you and their breath travels very far and very deeply; don't get contaminated by them, by their work, by their gesture, by their great

knowledge; they have great knowledge but be far away from them where

even you cannot find yourself. For they are waiting for you at every

corner, in every house to shape you, to mould you, to tear you to pieces

and then put you together in their own image. Their gods, the little ones

and the big ones, are the images of themselves, carved by their own mind

or by their own hands. They are waiting for you, the churchman and the

Communist, the believer and the non-believer, for they are both the same;

they think they are different but they are not for they both brainwash you,

till you are of them, till you repeat their words, till you worship their

saints, the ancient and the recent; they have armies for their gods and for

their countries and they are waiting for you, the educator and the

businessman; one trains you for the others to conform to the demands of

their society, which is a deadly thing; they will make you into a scientist,

into an engineer, into an expert of almost anything from cooking to

architecture to philosophy. Keep far, far away; they are waiting for you,

the politician and the reformer; the one drags you down into the gutter

and then the other reforms you; they juggle with words and you will be

lost in their wilderness. Keep far away; they are waiting for you, the

experts in god and the bomb throwers: the one will convince you and the other (show you) how to kill; there are so many ways to find god and so many, many ways to kill. But besides all these, there are hoards of others to tell you what to do and what not to do; keep away from all of them, so far away that you cannot find yourself or any other. You too would like to play with all of them who are waiting for you but then the play becomes so complicated and entertaining that you will be lost. You should never be here too much, be so far away that even you cannot find yourself.

J. Krishnamurti

Mike and I moved out of Sedona to Jerome. This was an even smaller town with about 400 people. We were renting this house on the hill with views all the way to Flagstaff; it was quite beautiful. Three months later we moved out of Jerome and down to Cottonwood, into this quaint little house. Downsizing felt so good, dumping all of the baggage we had been storing up for the past five years. I still get restless, I still drink too much and I still smoke but I don't care anymore. I'm okay with it all; okay with going with the flow and living this very short existence. Once in a while I get caught up in some human dramas, then it's over as soon as it started. Nothing lasts too long. I don't feel guilty about anything and I surely do not live with any regrets. Mike and I are sharing our lives together. He is an amazing man and I am thrilled he has decided to take this ride with me.

It goes so fast, this thing called life and I do get tired. I can't seem to figure it out. Maybe there is nothing to figure out. It's not the struggles, the roller coaster ride of life; it's the human race. People. I can barely stand to be around people anymore. So self absorbed, so greedy. People don't realize that this life will end someday. We assume we have the next moment and we go on taking all we can take, fucking each other over all for our own gain, and for what? We hoard and protect what we can never own. More is better and we work endlessly to have the bigger house, the nicer cars, all of the amenities to make our lives more bearable, but do they?

It never ends and I make no difference. I have thought of so many ways to do it. I tried to overdose on pills; I could put a plastic bag over my head. Hanging myself was a thought. I could fall asleep in a bathtub. I have had so many thoughts on ending this life. I don't see anything wrong with ending my life. It's my life and I can do whatever I want with it! Some people may disagree by saying it's a selfish act, but is it? What's selfish

245

about it? That I would leave this world and leave my loved one's behind to morn? Would the ones that love me rather I stay and struggle right along with them? Put up with all of the shit? I really feel that no one cares anyway; I would love to believe that they do but I'm only fooling myself. Most people are in it only for what they can gain from it and when the chips are down they are nowhere to be found. Outside of Mike, I can't remember a real conversation with a so-called loved one. It's such a sad joke really. So, who besides Mike would really give a fuck if I left this planet? I used to think I could make a difference. It was so important to me to be validated. I would do anything to help someone out and no matter how many times I got burned I would still do it! I didn't want to be a hard or bitter person. I use to hear that I never learned from my mistakes and until I did I would keep repeating them. I don't believe in mistakes. There is no right or wrong; I do what I do and move on. To not help another because I was burned in the past is silly and I won't live my life that way! I must say this life has been interesting. All of the drama, all of the relationships, the ups, the downs; and here I am, 43 years old. I still have my Buddha cat Schekki. I finally found the love of my life. I'm finally realizing that I can't find happiness, I can't find security, and I can't find or search for anything! It's the nothingness – the realization of that. I am NO-Thing and in the understanding of that there is this emptiness. Crazy shit really; hard to grasp I'm sure. Here I am, breathing in and out and I suppose when that stops, it stops. But it won't be by my hand. When you realize that nothing matters then, magically, everything matters.

So, you ask what has changed? Nothing and everything. In the days when I would try to force change and cry when I didn't get my way I now see it. I see how everything fits and that I never did have any control. One thing could not have happened without the other thing. It really is amazing when you look back through it all and see how it all comes together. And what does it mean? Nothing, absolutely nothing!

www.ingramcontent.com/pod-product-compliance
Lightning Source LLC
Chambersburg PA
CBHW022015090426
42739CB00006BA/141